The Survival Guide

for

Marriage in the Military
For Dating and Married Couples

Revised Edition

Gene Thomas Gomulka

A PlainTec Production
PlainTec Publishing
Groton, Connecticut

For information address:
PlainTec Publishing
8 Heron Lane
Groton, CT 06340

www.plaintec.net

Library of Congress Cataloging-in-Publication Data
The Survival Guide for Marriage in the Military:
For Dating and Married Couples
Gene Thomas Gomulka
p. cm.

ISBN: 0-9748083-3-4

1. Marriage – Military – United States. 2. Marriage counseling
3. Marriage compatibility tests I. Title
Printed in the United States of America

To my wife
Leila,
and our twins,
Sasha Grace
and
Luke Alexander

CONTENTS

FOREWORD

I remember a day in 1988 on the island of Okinawa, where I commanded a regiment, when we were visited by the Marine Corps Commandant, General Al Gray. He and I stood together on a beach observing an amphibious landing exercise when General Gray said to me, "You know we just hit a major milestone in the Corps." I couldn't imagine what that was and I asked him about it. He said, "We now have more dependents than we have Marines for the first time in our history." I immediately caught the significance of that and could clearly see that the Commandant realized the importance of this fact for our service. The list of challenges for military leaders would only increase as a mainly single military establishment evolved into a predominantly married force.

Six years later, as the Commander of the First Marine Expeditionary Force (I MEF), I had an organization in which 43 percent of the force was married. The average grade in the forty-five thousand-man MEF was Lance Corporal (E-3). The Marine Corps has always been the youngest service by far and a service that constantly deployed and moved for operations, forward presence requirements, or training at a rate higher than any other service. It was not an organization that had the inherent stability conducive to making family life, relationships, and marriage easy. My first platoon as a young lieutenant in the mid sixties only had two of its 46 members married, my platoon sergeant and one of my sergeant squad leaders. I realized that a young lieutenant in my MEF in the nineties could easily have half of his unit married. Military marriage rates have risen over the years along with accompanying problems (e.g., divorce, abuse).

The All Volunteer Force created a compensation rate sufficient enough to encourage young military members to believe they are in good shape to marry and take on family and relationship responsibilities. The problem has been that the stresses of military life have actually grown worse. The military has had to catch up with the significant implications of this changing demographic (i.e., impact on family housing requirements, child care centers, marriage counseling, medical needs), and the rate of failed marriages among the young ill-prepared service members has grown in alarming proportion.

When I commanded a battalion at Camp Lejeune, North Carolina, I was blessed to have a dynamic young chaplain by the name of Gene Gomulka. He brought to the unit a tireless energy, a concern for the welfare of our Marines and Sailors, and a deep interest in preparing young service members for life's challenges. He was well experienced in marriage counseling from his pre-service parish duties, and he committed himself to understanding the unique environment of the military and how best to apply what he learned in his civilian pastoral environment. His remarkable success at connecting to the young Marines and Sailors greatly benefited the command in its ability to deal with individual problems before they became insurmountable. He could readily predict trends and emerging problems and recommend actions for us to take to head them off. As a result, the battalion led the division in fewest disciplinary problems to include Unauthorized Absences. His skills also brought him the trust, respect, and cooperation of the unit's commanders who clearly saw the value of his work.

Gene Gomulka continued on in a highly successful career as a Navy chaplain. In the course of that career he has developed numerous programs and publications to help young service members through difficult stresses and problems. He has especially focused on the problems of relationships and marriages. I know of no one else who has had the experience, drive, and passion to improve things in these critical areas that directly affect the readiness of our armed forces. His vast knowledge and extensive research on this subject make him further qualified to produce effective tools for commanders, chaplains and counselors to use in dealing with these issues. Gene's keen interest in helping our service men and women cope with, and understand, these crucial events in life have led him to develop, on his own time, a significant work on this vital subject. I am convinced that this insightful and innovative publication will be an important addition to every commander's kit bag of leadership tools – one that can profoundly impact the quality of marriage and family life in the armed services.

Anthony C. Zinni
General USMC (Retired)
November 10, 2004

PREFACE

In 2004, after completing 24 years of active duty service, I authored the first edition of *The Survival Guide for Marriage in the Military*. Unlike most marriage books that are designed to be read from cover to cover, *The Survival Guide* is an interactive work built around an inventory of eighty-two statements that partners complete and discuss with the help of counseling insights provided in the book. The insights, based on thirty years of pastoral counseling experience and input provided by hundreds of military couples, chaplains and family support counselors, are similar to the type of advice provided by counselors, therapists, chaplains and clergy that offer marriage preparation and enrichment counseling.

The publication of the first edition proved very successful. In addition to receiving numerous positive book reviews and customer feedback, the book was also endorsed by "Dear Abby" in her nationally syndicated column in which she wrote: [The Survival Guide] "is very well done, easy to read and jargon-free, and although it was written for military couples whose marriages can be subject to extreme stresses, it can provide food for thought to civilian couples as well."

This revised edition of *The Survival Guide for Marriage in the Military* contains significant amounts of new information, including insights gleaned from a weekly newspaper and website column I started following the book's publication. Similar to the first edition, it is unique in the following respects:

1. Unlike almost all marriage preparation and enrichment inventories, books and programs on the market today, *The Survival Guide for Marriage in the Military* is written primarily for military personnel and their family

members. Hence, many of the unique challenges faced by military families (deployments, frequent moves) that are not adequately explored in civilian works, are thoroughly addressed in this interactive military oriented publication.

2. While civilian pre-marital and marital inventories must be obtained from and graded by a professional, the inventory contained in *The Survival Guide* can be self-administered at home, at one's own convenience, without the time and travel involved in meeting with a counselor or member of the clergy.

3. Unlike most civilian inventories that can be costly, particularly those that require computerized grading and interpretation by a professional, this self-administered interactive program is far less expensive and more user-friendly.

4. Some people who complete inventories that are viewed and graded by others may sometimes be hesitant to be completely honest in their responses. *The Survival Guide,* graded by the couple themselves, guarantees confidentiality and encourages more honest responses than what are sometimes provided in professionally administered surveys.

5. The interpretation that is provided to couples that complete most marriage inventories represents the experience and insights of a particular counselor or clergy person administering the questionnaire. *The Survival Guide,* however, offers advice based not simply on the education or experience of one professional, but rather provides insights from literally hundreds of couples and professionals.

I regret that the large number of people who provided input into this work is too great to identify them all individually. Whatever good might come about as a result of this publication is a direct result of the insights provided by countless individuals and couples for whose assistance I will be forever grateful. Without their cooperation, contributions and encouragement, *The Survival Guide for Marriage in the Military* could never have come into being.

Gene Thomas Gomulka
January 2007

INTRODUCTION

More than half the people who serve in the armed services today are married. Unfortunately, more than half of those who marry while on active duty will divorce, many even before they complete their first term.

Although military divorce rates have always been higher than those in the civilian sector, military divorces have increased even more as a result of an increase in operational commitments following the terrorist attacks of September 11, 2001.

Why do so many military marriages fail? There are a number of reasons that include loneliness and stress caused by multiple long-term deployments and separations; financial insecurity particularly among junior enlisted personnel; immaturity on the part of service men and women who tend to marry much younger than their civilian counterparts; and the challenge of raising children from a previous relationship that predispose some families toward divorce. While some of these factors are not unique to couples in the armed services, the more of them that are present in a particular relationship, the harder it may be for that couple to achieve life-long marital happiness together.

While couples can benefit from a variety of civilian, religious or secular, marriage preparation and enrichment programs, anyone planning on marrying, or already married to someone on active duty, needs to appreciate the uniqueness of military life. This uniqueness includes both rewarding and challenging elements.

One of the rewards of serving in the armed services is the close, often life-long camaraderie that can develop as a result of sharing common hardships, particularly amongst those who have served together in combat. While a person in the civilian community can live next door to a neighbor for 20 years and know very little about that individual, a service man or woman can go through weeks of basic training or deploy overseas for a number of months and end up knowing someone so well that he or she becomes a friend for life.

Spouses who live in base housing, particularly if their partner is deployed, may often bond with a neighbor with whom they keep in touch even when they are no longer in the service. Another reward associated with serving on active duty is the opportunity to travel and to live not only in different states, but many different countries as well. It takes a spouse with "the right stuff" to be able to "hold down the fort" while one's partner is deployed. Yet, that same spouse might relish the fact that deployments or being stationed overseas can result in obtaining leather goods, crystal, jewelry, or other specialty items often unavailable or beyond one's price range at home.

If military life has its rewards, it also has its challenges. While military pay has improved greatly in recent years, it will never equal compensation offered in the private sector. It is for this reason that perfecting the art of financial management is crucial if marriages, particularly among junior enlisted personnel with children, are to survive.

Being gone for extended periods of time without the ability to come home for every situation (even the birth of one's child) requires a spouse who, helped by various family support agencies and highly effective command spousal support networks, can handle most situations on his or her own. Even with the availability of such assistance, however, the life of a military spouse can often be lonely. Loneliness, at both ends of the separation, can stress fidelity. A successful marriage depends on spouses who can deal with loneliness, particularly during deployments, while shoring it up with the pride that comes in the military from selfless service.

"Serving in the military" and "having a job" are similar, but also very different. While one is often free to quit one's civilian job and seek other employment, those who serve in the military cannot wake up one morning and simply decide to quit. Even though a number of men and women do not complete their first term, most people who enlist fulfill their obligations and leave the armed services far more mature, educated and trained than they were when they first took an oath to "defend the Constitution of the United States."

The need to mold personnel into a "fighting team" requires an appreciation of teamwork far greater than in the majority of non-military "jobs." This, however, sometimes creates stress between the reasonable demands of married life and team membership. For example, if a service member misses an operation because of family demands, the lives of other team members of his unit may be at risk when they are deprived of that person's particular expertise. It is unfair for spouses of service members to complain that their partners cannot take advantage of "personal time" and "sick days" that their civilian friends and neighbors by be afforded by their employers. An understanding military spouse must recognize that devotion to one's unit is a key ingredient that can "bring them back alive."

In addition to military chaplains and family support counselors that provide counseling services, senior non-commissioned officers can also be effective in helping subordinates deal with relationship problems that can have long-term serious consequences. For example, a 19 year-old private or seaman who is planning to marry a girl in her mid-teens, or a much older woman with children from previous relationships, is a marriage disaster waiting to happen. Many senior enlisted personnel and junior officers recognize how some of their subordinates may be hesitant to seek the assistance of chaplains and counselors often out of concern for confidentiality. It is for this reason that many of them have recommended *The Survival Guide* as a confidential relationship tool that will not be viewed by their personnel as a threat to their careers or security clearances.

The book is built around "Statements" that partners are asked to respond to and discuss with the aid of counseling insights designed to promote happier marriages and reduce the chances for divorce. The statements are divided into nine categories that address the most critical aspects of married life. While this is not a test to calculate marital success, it can prove helpful in identifying specific issues that couples need to examine in greater detail in order to deepen their love for one another.

Only a small percentage of young people who marry while on active duty receive pre-marital instructions. Even fewer military couples complete marriage inventories that can be costly and require professional administration. The relationship inventory in this book, designed for both dating and married military personnel, does not require the initial professional involvement of a counselor, chaplain or member of the clergy. Further, unlike civilian marriage inventories that tend to be broad in their treatment of marriage and family life, this one addresses the major areas of married life in the context of the unique circumstances and challenges of military service.

The bottom line is that people who plan on marrying, or are already married, while one or both partners are on active duty, need to come to grips with the unique circumstances of military life that impact their relationship. Couples interested in evaluating the depth of their relationship and in deepening their love for one another can benefit greatly from this book that provides insights offered by hundreds of military couples, chaplains, counselors and clergy.

INSTRUCTIONS

Remove the "Statements" on pages 133-144. In a quiet place free from distractions, begin by reading the short introduction at the beginning of each category. Then read each statement very carefully. In the parenthesis before each number, respond to each statement with Y for "yes," N for "no," and U for "uncertain." You are strongly encouraged to respond "uncertain" if for any reason you find that a simple "yes" or "no" response might need to be qualified. The inventory's effectiveness is dependent upon each of you being radically honest in your responses. A lack of honesty can mask potential problems and decrease your chances for happiness by not having your expectations known and met.

Only after responding to all of the statements should you read the grading instructions at the end of the inventory that will inform you how to identify statements that represent potentially problematic issues worth discussing.

Once you have both graded your responses, make note of all the potentially problematic statements on the inventory found on pages 22-30. Place a check mark (√) in the parenthesis before each potentially problematic statement.

All the statements are intended for both dating and married couples. However, a few statements contain a phrase, preceded by a dash (–), that applies to those who are dating. This phrase is followed by a slash (/) and a phrase that is intended for married spouses (e.g., We have never had any arguments about – wedding plans / getting a divorce). Respond to that part of the statement that applies to your dating or marital status.

Once you have each responded to all of the statements, set aside some quality time to discuss the checked (√) statements that your self-grading process identified as potentially problematic. Before discussing a checked statement, first read the reflection for that particular statement found in the "Counseling Insights." The insights provided are similar to advice that one might receive from a professional that offers marriage preparation and/or enrichment counseling. The honest discussion that you have with your partner in regard to the potentially problematic statements is the most important part of this evaluation and enrichment process.

While some differences in opinion may be easily resolved, others may require more in-depth treatment, particularly if partners find themselves disagreeing over major issues. At the end of this discussion process, many partners will feel more in touch with each other's needs and deeper in their love for one another. Other couples, however, confronted with issues they are not able to resolve on their own, may need professional assistance to help them resolve their problems.

Some couples who discover a number of differences in certain areas may wish to enroll in programs designed to strengthen skills in particular areas of married life. For example, couples weak in finances or a spouse who has difficulty in controlling his or her temper, may wish to enroll in a budgeting course or in anger-management classes offered by the family support agency of their respective service. Additionally, many programs can be found advertised on the Internet that identify workshops, inventories, retreats and a host of marriage preparation and enrichment publications.

Couples who decide to seek professional help are encouraged to complete the "Biographical Profiles" found on pages 129-132. These profiles offer professionals important information that can enhance the effectiveness of the counseling they provide.

STATEMENTS

Unlike the detachable inventories on pages 133-144 that contain the responses of each partner, this inventory should be used to make note of those statements that the self-grading process identified as potentially problematic. Hence, consult your detachable inventories and place a check mark (√) before any of the following statements that one or both of you identified as potentially problematic.

COMMUNICATION

Effective communication is one of the most important factors of a successful relationship. When partners feel secure in their relation to discuss their feelings honestly, including their past disappointments, present concerns and future hopes, their chances of a happy life together are significantly enhanced.

( ) 1. *We have discussed how we will keep in touch when military requirements (e.g., deployments) force us to be separated. (33-35)*

( ) 2. *Our communication skills could not be better (e.g., we never nag or employ the "silent treatment"). (35-37)*

( ) 3. **My partner could be more sensitive in offering me encouragement and support when I am discouraged or depressed. (37-38)**

( ) 4. *My partner apologizes without hesitation after doing something wrong or hurting me. (39-40)*

( ) 5. *My partner usually talks with me when there is something on his/her mind. (40-41)*

( ) 6. **My partner seems uncomfortable at times in sharing his/her deep feelings with me. (41-42)**

( ) 7. **I am sometimes uncomfortable in asking my partner for what I would like or want. (42)**

( ) 8. **I am unhappy at times with the way decisions are made in our relationship. (42-43)**

( ) 9. *We enjoy stimulating conversations on a broad variety of matters. (43-44)*

( ) 10. **We were living together before we became engaged. (44-45)**

CONFLICT RESOLUTION

The success or failure of marriages is often determined by the way couples handle differences and conflicts that inevitably arise. Relationship problems are generally compounded when partners try to resolve them by employing destructive techniques (e.g., screaming, physical abuse, threats, name-calling, silent treatment). The ability to negotiate and resolve conflicts through constructive dialogues marked by mutual respect is an art worth perfecting.

( ) 1. *I generally feel satisfied with the outcome of our arguments. (47-49)*

( ) 2. *We are usually able to resolve our problems without revisiting the same issues over and over again. (49-50)*

( ) 3. **My partner sometimes fails to control his/her anger. (50-51)**

( ) 4. *I usually can sense when and know why my partner may be upset with me. (51-52)*

( ) 5. *We are able to avoid arguments over petty matters. (52)*

( ) 6. **We sometimes bring up mistakes that were made in the past. (53)**

( ) 7. **I am a little concerned about how a past abusive or unfaithful experience might adversely affect our relationship. (53-54)**

( ) 8. **We sometimes fail to handle conflicts in constructive ways (e.g., by yelling or screaming). (54-55)**

( ) 9. *My partner has never criticized me in public. (55-56)*

( ) 10. *My partner and I would not hesitate to seek counseling if problems developed and persisted that threatened our relationship. (56-57)*

DOLLARS AND SENSE

One of the principal reasons for discord among military couples involves finances. Conflicts can often arise over how a couple's income is managed. In order to avoid serious problems involving finances, couples are urged to adhere to a budget that reflects their mutually agreed upon priorities.

( ) 1. *We are familiar with our income and expenses and are committed to maintaining and following a budget. (59-60)*

( ) 2. *We pay our bills on time and we agree upon who will be/is responsible for paying them. (60-61)*

( ) 3. **I don't know exactly how much my partner makes and spends. (61-62)**

( ) 4. *I trust my partner completely with all of our money (e.g., checkbook, credit cards). (62)*

( ) 5. **I am uncomfortable that partner earns more than me. (63)**

( ) 6. **We have yet to decide how much we can each spend without consulting one another. (63-64)**

( ) 7. *After having discussed savings, investments, debts, assets, powers of attorneys and wills, we believe we have a sound plan for our future financial security. (64-65)*

( ) 8. **We have yet to decide about the types and amount of insurance to carry (e.g., life, health, car, home). (65)**

INTIMATE RELATIONS

Love can be expressed in a very fulfilling and meaningful way through our sexuality. While partners can experience a deep sense of intimacy from physical expressions of their love, sexuality can also be a source of frustration and anxiety. An honest sharing of one's feelings about sex can enhance a couple's appreciation of how their sexuality can complement their love for one another.

( ) 1. *My partner exceeds all of my expectations for love and affection. (67-69)*

( ) 2. *My partner and I are comfortable in talking about sex. (69-70)*

( ) 3. *I am not worried that my partner has been or will be unfaithful. (70-72)*

( ) 4. **I am sometimes uncomfortable with the way my partner relates to members of the opposite sex. (72)**

( ) 5. **I sometimes wonder if my partner's interest in me is primarily sexual. (72-73)**

( ) 6. **I sometimes worry about how my partner's past sexual relationships might have physical or other consequences in our lives. (73-74)**

( ) 7. *Our relationship could end if one partner were to be unfaithful. (74-75)*

( ) 8. *There are no homosexual feelings on my part or on the part of my partner. (75)*

( ) 9. *I can easily identify at least ten different ways of maintaining intimacy and not losing romance in our relationship. (76-77)*

( ) 10. *I am very well informed of various physical and psychological problems that can affect a decrease in a person's sex drive. (77-78)*

TODDLER STRATEGIES

People come from many different family backgrounds -- large families, small families, healthy families and even broken families. From these backgrounds often arise ideas of how people envision the home they are about to build. Couples need to discuss their family vision and their respective responsibilities in regard to having and raising children.

( ) 1. *We are in complete agreement about our desire to have (more) children. (79-80)*

( ) 2. **We are not in total agreement about the size of family we would like to have. (80-81)**

( ) 3. **We disagree about when we would like to have (more) children. (81-82)**

( ) 4. *We are in agreement about methods of family planning. (82-83)*

( ) 5. *We agree about how we will raise and discipline our children. (83-84)*

( ) 6. **We have different views on adopting children. (84-85)**

( ) 7. **We differ in our views on abortion. (85-86)**

( ) 8. *We know how to help children cope with the separation of a parent (e.g., during deployments). (86-87)*

( ) 9. *I am familiar with the positive and negative effects children can have upon a couple's relationship. (87-88)*

IN-LAWS, OUTLAWS AND OTHERS

Our relationship with our families and friends changes in some ways once we are married. While husbands and wives need to be best friends, they also need good friends and family members to support them throughout their married lives.

( ) 1. *Both of our families are supportive of our relationship. (89)*

( ) 2. **My partner's family at times becomes too involved in our relationship. (89-90)**

( ) 3. **I am uncomfortable with some of my partner's friends. (91)**

( ) 4. **I am concerned about the degree of my partner's involvement with some of his/her friends. (91-92)**

( ) 5. **I am hesitant to share with my partner some emotional hurts I experienced in my life (e.g., abuse, broken relationships). (92-93)**

( ) 6. *My partner is very sensitive to any relational or emotional problems I may have experienced in the past. (93)*

( ) 7. *We both have made a number of good friends and have similar and complementary interests. (93-94)*

( ) 8. *We have a healthy balance between the time we spend together, the time we spend alone, and the time we spend with family and friends. (94-95)*

( ) 9. **Some people questioned that we - may be marrying / married – too soon. (95-97)**

( ) 10. *We have discussed the possibility of a parent living with us if the need were to arise. (97-98)*

GREAT EXPECTATIONS

Past performance is often an indicator of future behavior. Recognizing that people are not changed by a wedding ceremony, partners need to honestly discuss their likes and dislikes in the present, as well as their hopes and dreams for the future.

( ) 1. **I wish I knew more about my partner's past so I don't have to worry about how my partner might act in the future. (99-100)**

( ) 2. *My partner and I are in agreement about leaving or staying on active duty, and we have discussed what we might do after we leave military service. (100-101)*

( ) 3. *I am satisfied with how we have decided to divide our various household tasks (e.g., cooking, cleaning, paying the bills). (101-102)*

( ) 4. *We have discussed and are in agreement about the issue of both partners working. (102-103)*

( ) 5. *We have never had any arguments about - wedding plans / getting a divorce. (103-104)*

( ) 6. *We are in agreement about what kind of home we would like to have and can afford to buy. (104-105)*

( ) 7. **We cannot seem to agree about our future career plans. (105-106)**

( ) 8. **Our ages are a concern to some family members and friends. (106-108)**

( ) 9. **I have some doubts about - marrying / staying married to - my partner. (108-109)**

( ) 10. *We are well prepared to deal with any number of tragedies in the future. (109-110)*

DIVINE INTERVENTION

Individual and shared religious views can have a major impact upon marriage and family life. Studies show that shared religious practice contributes to higher degrees of marital happiness and reduces the chances of divorce. A couple's spirituality affects not only their own lives but also the lives of their children and those around them.

( ) 1. *We are in agreement about where – we will marry / we were married (i.e., in a civil ceremony or in a particular religious service). (111-112)*

( ) 2. *I understand how a couple's moral and religious values can affect their marital success and happiness. (112-113)*

( ) 3. **We have yet to agree upon the role of religion in our relationship (e.g., attending worship). (113)**

( ) 4. **We have unresolved questions about the religious upbringing of our children. (113-114)**

( ) 5. *I am satisfied with my partner's attitude toward my religious beliefs and practices. (114)*

MISCELLANEOUS

Statements in this area address leisure time, public behavior, personal habits, household concerns, foreign relationships and second marriages. While we may accomplish some changes on our own (e.g., stop smoking, go to school, lose weight), certain addictions may require professional help if they are to be arrested (e.g., drug addiction, spousal abuse, alcoholism). The challenges of marrying a foreign national, or being married for a second or third time, might also require special assistance and counseling.

( ) 1. **I wish my partner spent less time on the computer, watching DVDs or television. (115-116)**

( ) 2. *I have never been embarrassed to be seen with my partner in public. (116)*

( ) 3. *We agree about how neat and clean our home should be kept. (116-117)*

( ) 4. **I am concerned about some of my partner's habits. (117-118)**

( ) 5. *We are in agreement about the presence of pets around the house. (118-119)*

( ) 6. **I wish my partner were more attentive in remembering special occasions and acknowledging them in special ways (e.g., cards, flowers, gifts). (119-120)**

( ) 7. *We were both born in the United States. (120-121)*

( ) 8. **One (or both) of us was married before. (121-122)**

( ) 9. *We are both ethnically, racially, and linguistically the same. (122)*

( ) 10. *We are thoroughly briefed on the problems that can arise following a deployment. (123-124)*

COUNSELING INSIGHTS

COMMUNICATION

Effective communication is one of the most important factors of a successful relationship. When partners feel secure in their relation to discuss their feelings honestly, including their past disappointments, present concerns and future hopes, their chances of a happy life together are significantly enhanced.

1. We have discussed how we will keep in touch when military requirements (e.g., deployments) force us to be separated.

One of the most challenging aspects of married military life involves being separated from family and loved ones for extended periods of time. While separations can have a positive effect in preventing some partners from taking one another for granted, they can also negatively affect the commitment of other dating and married couples. Communication during these periods of separation is vitally important.

Couples should employ personal, effective and economical ways of communicating with one another during these periods. Options may vary depending upon location. Some partners have developed serious financial problems as a result of making lengthy long-distance phone calls from abroad or by using cell phones exceeding the number of free minutes associated with a particular calling plan. Although international phone rates have decreased in recent years, one young man spent more than $10,000 for phone calls while working overseas. Unfortunately, his excessive phone calls contributed to serious financial problems that led to the dissolution of his relationship. Consequently, many couples place limits on overseas phone calls and are attentive to their balance of cell phone minutes.

A common and economical way of communicating today is via email or meeting in a chat room. Studies have shown that email boosts morale, increases confidence and self-assuredness throughout the separation, provides greater emotional connectedness with loved ones, and facilitates reunion and reintegration that can prove challenging following particularly long-term separations. While email is faster and more economical than the postal service, some couples feel that hand-written letters or cards on anniversaries and special occasions are more meaningful and appreciated than electronic communications.

Couples who mail letters almost daily to each other during deployments know the importance of numbering their envelopes. Mail can sometimes be delayed, and misrouting can cause letters to arrive out of order.

Operational security (OPSEC) may at times preclude sending or receiving postal or electronic mail. Hence, the lack of communication should not be construed as a lack of love. A number of valid reasons may exist why a partner is out of touch for a period of time. If there is a serious problem, one can ordinarily expect to receive an American Red Cross message or to be contacted by a command representative. Prior to deployments, family members should be well informed of how to contact their military loved ones in cases of emergency.

Some couples also communicate by video or audiotapes. One father purchased books for his children that he would read aloud and record. When the children were tucked in for the night, their mother would turn the pages of the book while playing the audio cassette. Although their father was thousands of miles away, his voice proved very comforting and assuring to both his wife and children.

Many commands will arrange video taping sessions or teleconferencing to allow service members and their loved ones to communicate during long deployments.

The frequency of communications during deployments will vary according to circumstances and events both at home and with the deployed command. Family responsibilities, particularly if there are small children at home, can affect the ability of a person to communicate as much as he or she might like. Some partners have more free time to communicate than others. Hence, one should not judge a partner's commitment by the number of letters or e-mails that others might receive.

Partners should not write while they are angry. While communications during extended periods of separation can enhance relationships, they also have the potential to weaken relationships. If a partner becomes upset, he or she should calm down and give more thought to a particular matter before pushing the "send" button or mailing the letter.

Have you been separated from each other for more than six months at a time? Have separations weakened your love, or have they helped you appreciate one another all the more? Do you attempt to communicate daily when you are separated from one another?

2. Our communication skills could not be better (e.g., we never nag or employ the "silent treatment").

Effective communication requires both a speaker and a listener. If both partners are speaking and neither is listening, real communication is not taking place. Communication requires that one person speaks and the other person really listens.

It is very helpful, particularly when partners may be at odds over a particular issue, that one partner repeat in his/her own words what he/she heard the other partner say. Such repetition can help reduce misinterpretations and let one partner know that the other partner is really interested in what he or she really feels.

Rather than being accusatory (e.g., "You always..." or "You are just like your..."), partners should share personally how they feel about a particular situation (e.g., "I feel like I'm being taken for granted when..."). Such an approach can improve communication while at the same time effectively reduce conflict.

Some people find that they can better express their feelings through written rather than spoken words. Although effective communication implies using verbal skills, writing a note to one's partner to express one's feelings may enhance communication and strengthen love.

Men are prone to employ the "silent treatment" when there is a break-down in communication. Unfortunately, this does not ordinarily contribute to a joint resolution of problems. While there is a time for speaking and a time for remaining silent, one woman discovered that if she refrained from being "pushy" and gave her partner some "space," her partner was more inclined to discuss an issue with her after having been given some time to reflect upon it.

While men have traditionally been portrayed as confrontational warriors and women have been viewed to be less aggressive, the opposite is often true in the realm of human relations. Women tend to be more willing and determined to address an issue, while men tend to withdraw and avoid confrontation. Unfortunately, this can create an unhealthy cycle in which the woman only becomes pushier, causing the man to retreat all the more. By understanding these differences, women can take steps to become less contentious and men can try to become less withdrawn when faced with a given problem.

Some people can express themselves on a deeper emotional level through writing than they can through speaking. For example, many military personnel have testified that despite being separated from their loved ones for 6-12 months at a time, they have actually grown in their love as a result of their daily emailing and letter writing. So too have many civilian couples found that writing and discussing notes and letters at convenient times have enhanced their communication and strengthened their relationships.

Some couples find it easier to communicate while walking or otherwise not facing each another. Direct eye contact may make some people reluctant to be totally open because of fear of confrontation or submissiveness.

Communication opportunities can be affected by work schedules and involvement in children's activities. One way to maintain good communication is by agreeing to have at least one meal together at table and not in front of the television. In this way at least one opportunity for meaningful dialogue will be available every day.

Are you able to chat naturally at different times and places about stimulating topics that bring you closer together, or do you find conversation difficult and centered on mundane issues? Does your partner interrupt you instead of listening and allowing you to speak? Do you pay more attention to the television instead of your partner? Do you or your partner employ the "silent treatment" in an attempt to avoid confronting a particular issue? Unless problems are addressed and discussed, they will often not go away but only grow worse. Consequently, couples should avoid delaying discussion of a troubling issue for too long lest a minor problem evolve into a major one.

3. My partner could be more sensitive in offering me encouragement when I am discouraged or depressed.

There are certain times in our lives when we need more love and support than what we might ordinarily require. Examples of such circumstances can involve pregnancy, the death of a loved one, health or financial problems, moving to a new home, having a new child or starting a new job. It is important that we communicate our willingness to compensate for our partner when such circumstances arise.

When we find ourselves down and out, it may require a statement on our part to let our partner know that we are hurting or in need of a good hug. Human beings are not mind readers. Consequently, we cannot always know what another person is thinking or feeling. Rather than feeling that our partner doesn't care about an issue that may be troubling us, it is best that we speak up and ask for the support and encouragement that we would like to receive.

It is important to note that men and women view support in different ways. While men often prefer a few encouraging words, women often need consolation accompanied by physical affection. Women are also more likely to call upon relatives and friends for additional support in times of crisis. Because men tend to be more reluctant to share their feelings, they may not always understand why their partner may share her problems with others.

While it is unfortunate when one partner is discouraged or depressed, it is even more problematic when both partners may be down and out for whatever reason. Under such circumstances, the ability to communicate one's feelings and needs is all the more important.

How well do you share your feelings with one another? Can you sense when your partner is upset or preoccupied about something without anything being said? Would you like you partner to be more expressive of his or her feelings? Are you jealous of your partner's abilities, or do you frequently tell others about his/her talents and accomplishments? Do you affirm one another by paying each other compliments (e.g., "That meal was awesome" or "You look absolutely gorgeous")?

4. My partner apologizes without hesitation after doing something wrong or hurting me.

Most people know that the movie line "love means never having to say you're sorry" doesn't apply to real life. We all disappoint and upset one another from time to time. There are even times when we hurt one another without even realizing it. Whether the hurt we caused was intentional or not, we need to be able to say, "I'm sorry." These two words only serve to reinforce three other words we may not say as often as we should: "I love you."

One chaplain friend teaches couples to adhere to five steps when dealing with hurt:

1) Verbalize your feeling ("I feel hurt when you…")
2) Explore motives ("Why did you..?)
3) Apologize ("I'm sorry that I…")
4) Forgive ("I forgive you…")
5) Put the matter to rest and do not bring it up again.

Some people find it hard to apologize or to admit that they did something wrong. When we fail to apologize, we in effect are saying, "I didn't do anything wrong." However, when we say, "I'm sorry," we demonstrate that we want to learn from our mistakes and thereby grow in the process.

In addition to asking for forgiveness, making amends may also be in order. If my son accidentally were to break a neighbor's window, apologizing for not being more careful needs to be followed by steps to have the broken window replaced at my son's expense.

As the chaplain noted in his "Five Steps" above, in addition to apologizing, we also need to forgive. Relationships cannot endure if partners do not practice forgiveness. People who dwell on past hurts, seek retribution, and fail to forgive, often end up hurting themselves both mentally and physically. Once forgiveness is offered, the incident that triggered the hurt should not be brought up at a later date.

If forgiveness is not immediately forthcoming after an apology has been rendered, patience may be in order. Some people take a little time to get over their hurt. Eventually, however, a sincere apology will move most people to forgive and, hopefully, forget.

Do you apologize even when you unintentionally hurt your partner? Could you see yourself or your partner saying, "I'm sorry I worried you when I didn't call to let you know I'd be home late"? How long does it ordinarily take for you to "kiss and make-up" when you have had a disagreement? Have you both demonstrated an ability to "forgive and forget" in your relationship?

5. My partner usually talks with me when there is something on his/her mind.

The better partners are able to communicate their hopes and desires, and the sooner they are able to resolve any differences, the stronger their relationship will be. A husband returned home one day from work and was told by his wife that she was considering leaving him. He was caught completely off-guard by her remark. While they may not have had a perfect marriage, he certainly didn't believe it was so bad that his wife would consider a divorce. Was it his fault for not listening to his wife's concerns, or was his wife ineffective in communicating her dissatisfaction with aspects of their relationship?

At the time of their marriage, one couple decided they would never go to sleep angry with one another. Another couple discovered, however, that problems are best discussed outside of the bedroom. Small problems can become big problems if they are not addressed within a reasonable amount of time.

Do you give your partner time to work out certain issues by affording him or her some "space" complemented by your patience and support? When you want to talk with your partner about something that is of concern to you, do you identify a time when you can sit down and discuss this matter together? With the goal of wanting to exceed your partner's expectations, would you like your partner to be more articulate in sharing his or her likes and dislikes?

6. My partner seems uncomfortable at times in sharing his/her deep feelings with me.

Intimacy in a relationship is enhanced when the partners share their hopes, fears, joys and sorrows. The more we open up and become vulnerable to our partner, the more we allow that person to love us. Some people go through life together in a relationship that at best can be termed "superficial." Other couples achieve an intimacy that only grows deeper as they journey together through life. While we each need a certain amount of privacy in our lives, such "space" should serve to complement the intimate sharing we enjoy with the most important person in our lives.

Partners who are hesitant to share their feelings risk being misinterpreted. When a husband became very upset after his favorite sport's team lost a game, his spouse misinterpreted his bad mood as being the result of her not being affectionate enough with him. She then began to wonder if he might be having an affair. Even after she questioned his perceived unhappiness and he told her about his team's loosing streak, she still wondered if he invented that excuse in an effort to cover a more serious problem. Had he been more transparent in sharing his feelings, the misinterpretation could very well have been avoided.

A number of couples find that there are times and places when they are more relaxed and conversant in sharing their feelings. For some it may be at meal time, while for others it may be after dinner. When do you find yourselves most relaxed in sharing what is on your mind or in your heart? Are there distractions in your lives (e.g., television, the Internet) that prevent you from being more effective in communicating on a deeper level with one another? What specific steps would you like to take to improve your communication (e.g., limit the number of times you have dinner while watching television or a movie)?

7. I am sometimes uncomfortable in asking my partner for what I would like or want.

Most of us would like our loved ones to anticipate our needs and provide us with what we would like without having to ask for it. That's fine, if our loved ones can read our minds. Our partner may find it difficult to meet our needs if he or she doesn't have a clue what we really want. It is better to communicate our expectations with our partner lest our disappointment weakens our relationship or moves us to find satisfaction with someone else.

About half of all the marriages in the United States end in divorce, and only a little over half of those who are not divorced would say they are happily married. How many of those people who are not happily married could be happier if they only asked for what they find lacking in their marriage? How would you respond to your spouse if he or she asked, "What can I do to exceed your expectations?" It may take a third party, perhaps even a counselor or therapist, to help a couple determine if certain requests are reasonable or excessive.

8. I am unhappy at times with the way decisions are made in our relationship.

Decision-making can be demonstrative as to who is in charge or responsible. When partners share responsibility for making decisions, no one partner can either enjoy all the praise for a correct decision or suffer the blame for a bad decision. Consequently, it is important that decisions be made jointly, particularly involving financial matters and in situations dealing with children who may try to play one parent against the other.

If a partner feels he or she isn't consulted, particularly in regard to making important decisions (e.g., changing jobs or residences, purchasing a home or car), the strength of the relationship may be weakened. If a relationship is to last, both partners must feel good with the way important decisions are made in their relationship. In light of the fact that many couples find the first two years of marriage to be the hardest, it is important to develop good shared decision-making patterns early in the relationship.

Some couples have found it helpful to view decision-making in terms of plusses and minuses, with some analysis of alternatives. In that way the best decision may become apparent to both partners.

How are most decisions made in your relationship? Do you ordinarily attempt to reach a consensus together or does one partner attempt to dominate the decision making process? How much are you influenced in the way you make decisions by your respective upbringing experiences?

9. We enjoy stimulating conversations on a broad variety of matters.

A couple's ability to converse well together is one sign of a healthy relationship. When partners find they don't have anything to talk about, it may indicate that their relationship is heading for trouble.

Conversations can strengthen relationships by providing partners with new insights; by moving them to discover solutions to various problems; and by allowing them to gain a deeper understanding of each other's thoughts and feelings.

While topics of conversation may often include the news, family, friends and work, partners may also wish to discuss entertainment or vacation plans, past experiences, or even interesting encounters they had that day. Stimulating conversations often flow more freely when couples have shared interests and experiences. Finding an activity or hobby (golf, wine tasting, cooking) that both enjoy can foster these kinds of conversations.

When you converse together, do you believe your partner is a good listener and is generally very attentive to what you have to say? Is your partner genuinely interested in your activities and personal interests? Are there any topics you would prefer not discussing with your partner? Are there times when it seems more opportune to engage in a stimulating conversation (e.g., before dinner)?

10. We were living together before we became engaged.

Cohabitation rates have increased significantly particularly over the past 25 years. Many young adults view living together as a way to achieve the benefits of marriage and avoid the risk of divorce. Surveys reveal that most young people today believe that it is a good idea to live with someone before getting married.

Studies show that living together increases the risk of divorce, domestic violence for women, and physical and sexual abuse for children. Children of cohabitating parents are at higher risk of being abused than children living with married parents.

Couples who lived together before marriage have also been shown to have poorer communication skills in resolving problems than couples who did not previously cohabitate. The longer a couple cohabitates, the more likely they are of having a failed marriage.

Although there are problems associated with living together before marriage, research suggests that cohabitating for a short period of time with the person one intends to marry has no adverse affects upon the subsequent marriage. Consequently, cohabitation is least harmful when a couple is engaged and has identified a wedding date. Senior citizens and retired people who typically cohabitate rather than marry for economic reasons are likewise spared many of the problems encountered by cohabitating, marrying and divorcing young people.

If you and your partner have been cohabitating, have you considered living apart from one another to see what affect it might have upon your relationship? Do you know other couples who cohabitated before they became engaged and subsequently married? If so, are these couples to your knowledge happily married today?

CONFLICT RESOLUTION

The success or failure of a marriage is often determined by the way a couple handles differences and conflicts that inevitably arise. Relationship problems are generally compounded when partners try to resolve them by employing destructive techniques (e.g., screaming, physical abuse, threats, name-calling, silent treatment). The ability to negotiate and resolve conflicts through constructive dialogues marked by mutual respect is an art worth perfecting.

1. I generally feel satisfied with the outcome of our arguments.

No two people, regardless of how much they have in common, will agree on everything. There are certain issues that will surface from time to time upon which they will inevitably disagree. When this occurs, it is best that the partners "disagree without becoming "disagreeable." Ordinarily, neither partner is always right. Hence, a partner is somewhat arrogant to believe that he or she is never wrong. Compromise may be the best course of action to pursue instead of always trying to identify someone as the "winner." Regardless of who is right or wrong, the disagreement should end in an amicable manner.

Ultimately, compromising in a relationship is not giving in, but deciding what is important and gauging the importance of an issue with one's partner. The health of a relationship is much more important than winning an argument. The wise person will recognize when a given issue is more important to his or her partner, and will compromise, even though he or she may have other preferences or differing views.

Most couples, whether they are happy or not, will argue about certain issues. Some of the more common areas of disagreement involve finances, the division of household labor, children, and leisure interests. While some disagreements can involve minor issues such as where to dine or how high or low to set the thermostat, other disagreement may involve far more serious matters such as having children or infidelity on the part of one or both partners. In so far as most couples do not resolve the vast majority of their differences, marriage counselors will often attempt to help them live with them instead of always trying to solve them.

Some couples have found that "pre-planned responses" are beneficial in reducing conflicts. For example, many arguments arise due to the actions/behavior of in-laws, especially when one spouse expects the other to intervene with their "offending" parent. An agreement up front that each spouse will take appropriate action to deal with his/her own parents may prove very helpful.

Couples are encouraged to agree upon certain "rules of engagement" in regard to arguments. Such rules designed to help couples "fight fair" might consist of recognizing when the time is right or wrong to address an issue; listening without interrupting; speaking in a calm manner without raising one's voice; postponing the discussion if one or both partners are too upset; identifying what one might do to "cool down" (e.g., go for a walk); limiting the time allotted for a particular disagreement; discussing when to concede an impasse; having a mutually agreed upon list of items that are "off-limits" while engaged in the discussion (e.g., not bringing up the past, using foul language or putting down family members); being willing to compromise; and, when errors have been made, being humble enough to admit having made a mistake, asking for forgiveness, and being willing to forgive.

Have you considered developing certain "rules of engagement" to facilitate conflict resolution in your relationship? Have you discussed how you might handle some of the more common problems that couples experience before they occur in your own lives?

2. We are usually able to resolve our problems without revisiting the same issues over and over again.

If a person were to go to a doctor time and time again for a problem that just would not go away, one might begin to wonder if the doctor correctly diagnosed the problem. So, too, if partners continue to wrestle with the same problems, they may question their problem-solving techniques or wonder if the problem will ever go away. In so far as marriage is not a 50-50 proposition, there may not always be a solution to a particular problem. In such a situation, compromise is essential.

When disagreements arise, some partners may employ examples from the past in support of their position (e.g., "I'll never forget the time you…"). Such a tactic is seldom productive and often leads to escalation. It is far more productive to stick to the issue at hand and let past disagreements remain buried.

One father gave his daughter the following advice: "Before you get married, keep your eyes wide open. After you're married, keep them half-closed." While there are some things that we can change in our lives, there are other habits that we may never be able to change. If one partner has a serious problem (e.g., alcoholism, drug abuse, infidelity), the other partner has to question if he or she can accept this behavior throughout the course of their lives together. If the answer to that question is "no," the partners may need to seek professional help or risk the dissolution of their relationship.

Are there issues that you wish your partner would never bring up from the past? Are there certain problems that continue to resurface that just won't go away? Are there problems you feel will not be solved without professional help?

3. My partner sometimes fails to control his/her anger.

All couples experience conflicts and exhibit anger at different times in their lives. It's important that you learn how to resolve conflicts and manage anger; ask for forgiveness; be able to forgive; and know when it's time to seek professional help.

There are events that occur in our lives that can make us angry or depressed. Anger in itself is a normal human emotion. But anger that is directed toward someone in an excessive manner can prove destructive both for the angry individual and the object of that person's wrath. For example, a person can become angry if a reckless driver almost causes him or her to have an accident. Becoming excessively angry, however, does not justify pursuing the reckless driver and crashing one's car into that individual.

Anger is best directed toward actions and attitudes, and not toward people. Excessive anger can be manifested in various forms of abuse (e.g., verbal, spousal, child). Physical abuse is never acceptable and the cycle must be interrupted as early as possible. If one's partner is abusive, a loving response can involve getting out of the abusive situation or seeking professional help. Anger-management classes and other therapies can help arrest such behavior and reduce the chances of divorce, hospitalization of the victim of abuse, or even incarceration of the abuser.

Does the partner that cannot control his/her anger at times recognize and admit to having this problem? Has he/she ever discussed what might be the source of this problem (e.g., learned behavior from a parent)? What steps will be taken to prevent any form of abuse from harming or destroying your relationship?

4. I usually can sense when and know why my partner may be upset with me.

Good communication skills are a prerequisite to resolving conflicts. While some couples express their displeasure verbally, others resort to the "silent treatment." Rather than going to the extremes of yelling or becoming silent for an inordinate period of time, it is more productive to resolve problems by sitting down and calmly facing the issues at hand.

If one person doesn't communicate his or her dissatisfaction, and the other partner is not aware that a problem exists, the dissatisfied partner may only become more upset and be tempted to escape and employ unhealthy ways to fill the void in his or her life. Such escapes can include drug and alcohol abuse, sexual liaisons, working unnecessary overtime, sleeping excessively or leaving the house to avoid addressing issues. These escape mechanisms ordinarily only complicate the situation and turn what might be a minor problem into a major one.

Women are more prone than men to blame themselves if they believe their partner is unhappy. When a man comes across as uncommunicative, a woman may feel rejected. In reality, however, the man may be preoccupied with work or some matter unrelated to their relationship. In such circumstances, the man needs to reassure the woman that he is actually absorbed with other issues and that he really loves her.

Are you or your partner hesitant to express dissatisfaction with some aspect of your relationship? If this is true, what is the basis for the hesitancy? What does your partner say or do at times that leads you to believe that he or she is upset with you? Have you ever misinterpreted why your partner was upset about something before having learned the real reason?

5. We are able to avoid arguments over petty matters.

Disagreements over what music to listen to or what to have for dinner are far less important than whether or not to have children or where you will live and work. In recognizing that some issues are worth fighting for more than others, partners need to decide what matters are emotionally worth addressing.

A person can have a bad day at work, return home upset and argue over something insignificant as a way of "blowing off steam" to compensate for something that occurred earlier in the day. Here is where good communication skills can reduce arguments over relatively minor issues (e.g., "Something seems to be upsetting you, sweetheart. Is there something that happened today that you want to share with me?").

Unfortunately, because we sometimes take our loved ones for granted and use them as punching bags, we can be guilty of treating total strangers better than the people we love the most in the world. While this may happen to all of us at one time or another in our lives, it is something that we should seek to avoid.

Are empty ice cube trays or the TV remote control objects of contention in your relationship? Do you get upset when someone does not refill the toilet paper or leave the toilet seat in the down position? In a day and age of "equal rights," would it be a fair compromise to leave the toilet seat down half the time? Have you been hesitant to let your partner know what seemingly petty matters upset you? What are some "triggers" that set you and your partner off? What concrete steps will you both take to avoid "pushing the wrong buttons?"

6. We sometimes bring up mistakes that were made in the past.

We all make mistakes in our lives that we live to regret. When mistakes occur, often an explanation and an apology are offered, followed by forgiveness on the part of the offended party. If the problematic situation was not fully discussed, or if the unacceptable behavior continues to take place, then one shouldn't be surprised if the offended partner brings up this problem in conversation. This is particularly embarrassing when done in front of family or friends. However, if the issue was thoroughly addressed and there are no indications that the problem persists, then the offended partner should refrain from bringing up the matter that should once and for all be laid to rest.

The tendency to revisit problems may be a manifestation of a deeper problem in the relationship, and bringing up bad news from the past may just be the outlet. In such cases, it is important for the couple to address the root problem.

Healing cannot occur if old wounds continue to be opened up. Partners should allow healing to take effect by avoiding bringing up "sins" of the past. Forgiveness is not only appreciated by the person at fault, but it is also a gift to the one who was hurt. By practicing forgiveness we are unburdened from feelings of revenge, bitterness and hate that impact our own happiness.

Are there any particular "sins" that one partner brings up from time to time? If made aware of this practice, and if the issue is no longer problematic, can a resolution be made to bury it once and for all?

7. I am a little concerned about how a past abusive or unfaithful experience might adversely affect our relationship.

A partner who experienced abuse or infidelity in a family, dating or previous marriage relationship, sometimes has a tendency to transfer negative feelings to his or her partner, even though he or she had nothing to do with the past experience. Such negative feelings can weaken the relationship and prevent it from achieving its full potential. In order to help prevent this from happening, it's essential to distinguish between the past offender and the present partner who seeks a deep and loving relationship. Some people can make this distinction. Others may require professional counseling to help them come to grips with past abuse or infidelity, and then get on with their lives.

Are there "trigger events" from the past that need to be addressed lest they harm your relationship? Are you aware of bad experiences in your partner's past that may require hypersensitivity on your part lest you risk becoming the object of transference (i.e., the unconscious redirection of feelings about one person to another)?

8 *We sometimes fail to handle conflicts in constructive ways (e.g., by yelling or screaming).*

Some partners can tend to imitate their parents' behavior when it comes to resolving problems. For example, if a person comes from a home where his or her parents were physically or verbally abusive at times, that person may have a tendency to likewise resort to hitting or yelling whenever a problem arises. However, regardless of how one's parents resolved their differences, partners must agree that abusive methods are not only destructive to one another, but also to the psychological well-being of any children who might witness such abuse.

Partners who have never experienced any form of verbal or physical abuse may be particularly sensitive to being yelled at or hit. Partners need to discuss how their parents may have had an influence on their own approach to handling conflicts for better or for worse. They also would be wise to identify particular negative parental traits and vow not to imitate them. In one case, a man from a large family was accustomed to raising his voice when agitated, as it was the only way he could be heard in his crowded childhood. His partner, however, was an only child. She would burst into tears whenever he raised his voice, believing that he didn't love her. By discussing how they perceived yelling allowed them to understand each other better.

Do you raise your voice at times in an attempt to emphasize a point? Can you come up with a phrase your partner can use to let you know in a polite way that you need to calm down?

9. My partner has never criticized me in public.

Serious relationship differences and disputes are best settled in private. When one partner embarrasses the other by engaging in public criticism, he or she violates the intimate and exclusive bond of trust demanded in a mature and loving relationship. The offended party should address it directly and privately with a resolve between the two to avoid this method of expressing internal issues in public. Then both need to address the frustration that culminated in the public criticism. If this expression of frustration in public becomes habitual, counseling should be sought. Criticism of one parent by the other in the presence of children is particularly harmful, as it not only demonstrates a weakness of the marital bond, but also affects the psychological well-being of the children.

While some forms of teasing may not prove offensive, others that deal with a partner's weight, abilities, personal habits or sexual performance can be very hurtful. Lest a partner fail to cease making inappropriate comments or tasteless jokes, it is wise to confront this problem early by making it clear that such remarks are not funny and will not be tolerated.

If a person views the other partner as one's mate, and recognizes that they are both on the same team, personal attacks and hurtful or sarcastic remarks can be avoided. Rather than being adversaries, competitors and enemies, partners need to be mates, supporters and best friends.

Has your partner ever criticized or made fun of you in public? Has he or she ever told a joke or pulled a stunt that you found inappropriate or embarrassing? If this ever occurred, did you discuss it afterwards to prevent it from happening again?

10. My partner and I would not hesitate to seek counseling if problems developed and persisted that threatened our relationship.

If a person develops cold or flu symptoms, one ordinarily does not need to contact a physician. However, if a physical problem does not go away but becomes more serious, then most people would call upon a doctor for help. We don't need a physician to get over a cold, but we do need an oncologist if we are suffering from cancer. The same applies to relationships.

While the partners themselves can resolve some problems, other more serious problems require professional help from a counselor or trained civilian member of the clergy. Unfortunately, rather than seeking professional help, many dating and married couples seek advice from relatives, friends, co-workers and neighbors who generally are not capable or qualified to help them resolve their problems. Just as persons suffering from cancer do not go to other cancer patients for treatment, likewise, people with serious marital problems should not rely upon married or divorced acquaintances to solve their marital problems. We wouldn't think of asking a friend to remove our appendix, so why would we ask that same friend to operate on our relationship?

If your partner or you are hesitant to avail yourselves to counseling, is it because of fear? Are you afraid to admit that you cannot solve all of your own problems? Voluntarily seeking counseling is far better than having the problem grow worse and possibly destroying the relationship. When one partner refuses to pursue counseling, is the other partner justified in separating or seeking a divorce? How much unhappiness can one partner expect to endure before terminating the relationship?

Like most forms of cancer that have higher remission rates if treated early, so, too, can early detection and professional treatment of serious marital problems result in higher reconciliation rates leading to stronger and more fulfilling relationships. Just as one seeks the best doctor available, particular care should be given to finding a competent counselor.

DOLLARS AND SENSE

One of the principal reasons for discord among military couples involves finances. Conflicts can often arise over how a couple's income is managed. In order to avoid serious problems involving finances, couples are urged to adhere to a budget that reflects their mutually agreed upon priorities.

1. We are familiar with our income and expenses and are committed to maintaining and following a budget.

Many young military couples experience serious financial problems as a result trying to live beyond their means. In some cases, these problems become so severe that their relationship is dissolved. One way to prevent this from happening is to develop and adhere to a spending plan that prevents a couple from spending more than they make.

Whether one or both partners are employed and provide income to the household, the expenditure of that income affects the entire family. Consequently, financial decisions need to be made by both partners. In cases where both partners are employed, couples generally pool their incomes into one account to which they both have access. Selfishness (e.g., "this is my money") can spark many arguments and seriously weaken the relationship.

While one partner may have primary responsibility for paying the bills, both partners should be responsible for developing and following a budget. Books and classes on budgeting and financial-management are available to help couples spend and invest their money wisely. By reading these publications or attending such classes together, couples can develop a joint vision about how much they want to spend and how they want to invest their money.

Various military family support agencies offer budgeting and financial-management classes to help couples spend and invest their money wisely. By attending such classes together, couples can develop a joint vision about how much they want to spend and how they want to invest their money. While military couples receive certain entitlements to aid them and their children (BAH, VHA), such additional income cannot fully offset the additional expenses involved in raising a family. Free publications and information about financial management are also available through a number of governmental and non-governmental organizations.

Have you developed a budget based upon your income and expenditures? Do you have a clear idea of each other's assets and debts? Are your important documents (e.g., bank account and credit card numbers, insurance records, wills) kept in a secure location accessible to each of you? Have you discussed how you hope to achieve certain short-term and long-term financial goals for the future?

2. We pay our bills on time and we agree upon who will be/is responsible for paying them.

Partners have to decide not only how they will pay their bills (e.g., check, credit card, via the Internet), but also who will be responsible for carrying out this task. Some couples may have to reevaluate in time how they pay their bills and who carries out this task, particularly if they find themselves paying excessive interest charges or are assessed late penalties for not paying their bills on time.

While credit cards are a great convenience, they also tempt people to spend more than they can afford. Studies show that people spend two to three times as much with credit cards as they do with cash. Unfortunately, credit cards are a prime contributor to debt. It is hard enough to pay back the money one borrowed. It is even harder when one adds in interest and late payment fees.

Unfortunately, many people spend more money than they make and fall into a spiral of rising debt and increasing financial pressure. Debt is not only a financial problem, but it also the source of emotional problems that can affect one's physical and mental health. Symptoms of debt-related stress can include headaches, weight gain or loss, insomnia, anger and depression. Getting out of debt requires planning, time, discipline and sacrifices. It is difficult to get out of debt without adhering strictly to a detailed budget.

What partner is more talented in handling finances? Has one partner ever had a check bounce or incurred high interest charges on credit-card expenditures? If this has occurred in the past, what safeguards will the couple initiate to prevent this from happening in the future?

3. I don't know exactly how much my partner makes and spends.

Hesitancy to disclose all sources and amounts of income, as well as expenses, can be indicative of an unstable relationship and a source of mistrust. This situation should be addressed directly between the partners and resolved so that mutual trust can be recovered. Without mutual knowledge of a couple's income and expenses, adequate fulfillment of each other's household obligations, while not impossible, would be difficult at best and could very likely lead to financial difficulties.

When calculating income, it is best not to factor in "per diem" allocations that are provided to cover travel expenses. Arguments can ensue as to why these funds cannot be used to pay family bills. The lack of government lodging in certain areas where civilian accommodations and meals are expensive can easily consume "per diem" entitlements.

How much do you and your partner each make? What are your major recurring expenses (e.g., entertainment, clothing, hairdressing)? Only when the partners are completely aware of their financial status can they make wise decisions about where they can afford to live, what kinds of cars they can drive and what schools their children can attend.

4. I trust my partner completely with all of our money (e.g., checkbook, credit cards).

Financial trust presupposes faith and confidence in the present and future stability of the relationship. If a person feels that one's partner may break off the relationship in the future, that partner will not be inclined to afford complete and unlimited access to one's assets. The signing of a prenuptial agreement prior to marriage can also be indicative of a lack of confidence in the future viability of the relationship.

If a partner may be hesitant to grant complete access to all of his or her assets, it would be wise for that partner to discuss the reasons behind this hesitation. A person who feels that a partner might abscond some or all of their funds usually is dealing with a variety of other problems (e.g., lack of a life-long commitment, experiences of being cheated out of funds, infidelity).

In the case of second marriages where there are children from the first, some parents wish to ensure that any existing wealth prior to the second marriage is earmarked for those children in case he/she dies. Ordinarily, such a wish has nothing to do with lack of trust in the new spouse.

Do you both agree upon each partner having complete access to all funds? Do either of you have accounts or investments that you have not revealed to your partner?

5. I am uncomfortable that my partner earns more than me.

As more women enter into professional fields, a number of them may earn more money than their partners. While one person may be proud of his/her partner's accomplishments, another person man may be threatened by the other partner's financial superiority. In situations where conflict arises due to income differences, careful consideration should be given to the fundamental love relationship and the subordinate income relationship.

Financial income is only a means, and not an end, to meet our material needs. If financial income or career goals become ends in themselves, they can threaten a couple's relationship. In such cases, partners need to address this directly in such a way to protect the dignity of each individual while also strengthening their love and commitment.

Do you take pride in your partner's earning power and accomplishments or do you compete in wanting to equal or exceed his/her income? Does one partner equate making more money with being more important or contributing more to the relationship?

6. We have yet to decide how much we can each spend without consulting one another.

Some persons have lived alone for a number of years and have never had to consult with anyone about how much money they could spend. This way of operating financially changes when one marries. Some married couples establish a weekly allowance for miscellaneous expenditures and then discuss their bills jointly. Other married couples agree upon a monetary figure that each of them can spend without consulting one another.

By setting an amount that can be spent without consultation, one partner can be prevented from unintentionally putting the couple into debt. Agreeing upon such a figure is particularly helpful in cases where the partners do not come from similar financial backgrounds.

If one partner has more expensive tastes than the other, the couple may discuss what they can afford to buy and seek to compromise in regard to their divergent tastes. Additionally, if a particular partner has difficulty in adhering to a mutually developed budget, that partner should consult with the partner who has primary responsibility for the budget before expenditures are made.

How much do you each think you should be able to spend without consulting one another? Have you discussed how you may have to save a greater portion of your income(s) than you did when you were single to help cover additional future costs (e.g., expenses involved in having, raising and educating children)?

7. After having discussed savings, investments, debts, assets, powers of attorneys and wills, we believe we have a sound plan for our future financial security.

While some couples are very financially astute, others live from payday to payday without saving or investing money for the future. When an emergency arises, some couples are forced to take out a loan and later find themselves having to deal with high interest charges. Rather than being placed in this predicament, it's better to meet with a financial consultant and decide how to best invest surplus funds.

In addition to investing in stocks and bonds, some military couples have found that buying a home can be profitable in one area while financially disastrous in other areas. The less money a couple has to invest, the more conservative their investments should be.

Does each partner have a will? Are there debts that one or both of you bring to the relationship? Do you face an ongoing disbursement of funds (e.g., child support, mortgage or car payments)? Have you discussed your attitude about borrowing money from your parents? Are you familiar with the "Thrift Savings Plan" (TSP) and other governmental financial programs? Have you asked friends about a financial planner whom they have found to be helpful and successful in managing and investing their money? Have you discussed setting aside money for your children's education and your retirement?

8. We have yet to decide about the types and amount of insurance to carry (e.g., life, health, car, home).

Although military personnel are provided life insurance coverage in the event of death while on active duty, additional types of insurance may be procured by military couples (e.g., SGLI Plan). Various health plans are offered for military family members for various levels of medical and dental coverage. Supplemental coverage may be wise to purchase when special needs exist.

As changes occur in the lives of the partners (e.g., children are born, a new vehicle is purchased), insurance coverage will have to be adjusted accordingly.

Advice in regard to insurance coverage is available through some company personnel offices and a number of URL links.

Do you understand the differences between various types of life insurance (whole life, term life)? Do you believe you are sufficiently insured in all respects? Have you compared premiums charged by various companies for comparable coverage?

INTIMATE RELATIONS

Love can be expressed in a very fulfilling and beautiful way through our sexuality. While partners can experience a deep sense of intimacy from physical expressions of their love, sexuality can also be a source of frustration and anxiety. An honest sharing of one's feelings about sex can enhance a couple's appreciation of how their sexuality can complement their love for one another.

1. My partner exceeds all of my expectations for love and affection.

Couples vary in the ways they enjoy offering and receiving affection. Family attitudes, positive and negative experiences, psychological differences, religious teachings, cultural backgrounds, and physical factors all affect a person's attitude toward sexuality. The deeper a couple's love is for one another, and the better they can communicate their expectations, the greater appreciation and enjoyment they ordinarily derive from their sexual intimacies.

While studies show that men generally want more sex than women do, women need to feel emotionally connected before wanting to make love. Books that explore the psychological differences between men and women can often prove more helpful in enhancing a couple's sex life than those that merely address the purely physical aspects of love making.

Married and family life can become very hectic to the point where spontaneous sexual expressions of love may become fewer and farther in between. Couples who find this happening may have to schedule their sexual encounters lest other less important activities harm their relationship. Scheduling may be affected by their respective work schedules, as well as whether they are morning or night persons. Some couples set the stage in the morning by kissing and touching, think and even communicate during the day about what lies ahead, and bring the day to a close at night with a very intimate and even exhausting celebration of their love.

Men and women differ in regard to what turns them on sexually. Generally speaking, here are some ways men have found they are able to please women: create a romantic setting before getting between the sheets; be showered and smell great; don't rush foreplay; explore all of her erogenous zones; vary your sexual positions; allow her to reach orgasm first. When asked what seems to please men most, here is what a number of women recommend: wear sexy lingerie and remove it slowly; perform fellatio; tell and show him what pleases you; explore all of his erogenous zones; share your fantasies with him; do what you can to reach orgasm with him so as to reinforce his macho self-image.

Lack of sexual intimacy that includes both physical and emotional involvement can seriously threaten a marriage relationship. Couples who cannot resolve this problem on their own should consult a doctor or therapist before it leads to other problems (e.g., substituting pornography for marital relations, infidelity).

Many people have heard the expression, "The greatest gift a father can give his children is to love their mother." A couple's outward signs of affection can have a very positive influence on children. Conversely, witnessing a poor relationship may result in low self-esteem and can be an underlying cause of eating disorders and other problems among children. The value of a couple showing affection for one another in the presence of their children should not be underestimated.

Would you like to experience more hugs, cuddling and spontaneous kisses on a daily basis in your relationship? Have you honestly discussed each other's sexual expectations? Do you believe these expectations are realistic and attainable? Are you both aware of the many positive effects of regular sexual relations (e.g., decreases stress, burns calories, improves self-esteem, reduces coronary heart disease, enhances sleep, aids digestion, boosts the immune system, strengthens emotional bonds, increases longevity)?

2. My partner and I are comfortable in talking about sex.

A healthy sexual relationship can enhance the love a couple feels for one another. While positive experiences of love and affection can dispose one to more open attitudes toward sexuality, past negative experiences (e.g., incest or rape) can influence a partner to identify sexuality with lust and abuse rather than with intimacy and love. While some couples can work through past negative experiences that may have transpired at home or in a previous dating or marriage relationship, others discover that professional counseling may be necessary to alleviate fears and concerns rooted in the past. Discussions of sexuality that fail to recognize the critically important relationship between intimacy and sex can result in relegating sex to the realm of performance.

If talking about sex seems difficult for either partner, consider discussing various ways to enhance feelings of intimacy in your relationship. The more sex is viewed and appreciated as a vehicle for expressing love and experiencing intimacy, the less inclined a person might be to avoid talking about it.

Knowledge of certain basic differences that exist between men and women can increase the potential for sexuality to enhance the quality of a couple's love for one another. Reading books on relationships can help explain why many men feel intimate as a result of being sexual, whereas many women feel sexual as a result of being intimate. Literature in this field can help partners become more open and comfortable in discussing their feelings about their physical relationship.

Have you discussed with your partner various sexual expressions of love you would find pleasing and others in which you would prefer not to engage? Does your partner understand the different ways that men and women are aroused (e.g., verbally, visually) and how they may also be sexually "turned off" (e.g., by failing to connect emotionally)?

3. I am not worried that my partner has been or will be unfaithful.

Our concern about infidelity is conditioned in a variety of ways. For example, if one or both parents of a partner proved to be unfaithful, that person could have a heightened concern that his or her partner might also prove to be unfaithful. Additionally, if infidelity was personally experienced in a previous dating or marriage relationship, this might also move the person to question whether this behavior will be repeated.

If one or both partners are concerned about remaining faithful, this is a "red flag" that needs to be discussed. We can't control the behavior of our parents, former spouses or coworkers and their spouses. However, we can resolve that we will honor our promise when we say, "Take this ring as a sign of my love and fidelity."

People with whom we work and associate can influence our actions for better or for worse. Exemplary friends who epitomize what it means to be loving and faithful can motivate us to imitate their behavior and remain faithful for life. Promiscuous friends can have the opposite affect upon our lives.

A person who is suspicious that his or her partner may be sexually and/or emotionally involved with someone else may be tempted to spy by monitoring his/her partner's movements or by looking for evidence (e.g., phone records, email communications, credit card statements) of a possible affair. Such spying generally indicates a serious lack of trust that may or may not be warranted. Rather than spending a lot of money on hiring a private investigator, it might be wiser to secure the services of a qualified counselor with experience in these matters.

Before jumping to the conclusion that your partner may be unfaithful, consider if you believe your partner is capable of infidelity and if your suspicions might be unjustly motivated. While women's instincts in these matters are more often on target than those of men, it does not mean that a relationship cannot be saved even when infidelity occurs. The chances of saving a marriage affected by infidelity are increased if it is detected in an early stage and if both partners are willing to receive professional help in experiencing healing and restoring trust.

Couples who experience infidelity are advised not to act hastily in contacting a divorce lawyer on the assumption that the relationship is necessarily doomed to failure. Reactions can involve denial, anger, hurt and depression that can result in eating, sleeping and other physical and psychological problems. In these circumstances, couples are advised to be tested for sexually transmitted diseases including HIV/AIDS. Because the unfaithful partner may not always know why he or she was unfaithful, it is generally necessary to seek counseling in this regard. Once the reasons behind the infidelity are properly understood, it then becomes a matter of ascertaining if both partners not only wish to save the marriage, but also want to make it better. Because many marriages end in divorce that otherwise could be saved with professional help, couples are strongly advised not to make rash decisions that they may later live to regret.

What situation occurred in the past that might be the basis for one's concern about fidelity? Does one partner continually bring up a past unfaithful event, thus making it hard for the other partner to change? If your partner viewed or read pornographic material, might you interpret this as a form of unfaithfulness? Would you both be willing to seek professional help if you encountered serious problems in your marriage that you were not able to resolve on your own?

4. I am sometimes uncomfortable with the way my partner relates to members of the opposite sex.

It is difficult to build a life of love together if trust is lacking on the part of one or both partners. If one person is concerned about the way the other partner relates to members of the opposite sex, it may be due to a past experience of infidelity experienced or witnessed by the questioning partner.

It is healthy for men and women to have co-workers of the opposite sex that can help them develop an appreciation of the other gender's perspective. While some people are more affectionate than others, it is best that concerns along these lines be addressed and discussed honestly.

When one person is concerned about the other partner's friendships, is this a sign of insecurity, or is there a problematic relationship developing? Are there events that may have caused one person to be suspicious of the other partner (e.g., the manner in which a partner may have been dancing with someone, the degree of affection a partner may have demonstrated toward a co-worker)? Is there a problem in this area or is this merely a perception?

5. I sometimes wonder if my partner's interest in me is primarily sexual.

As sexual beings, we are sexually attracted to some people more than others. While sexual attraction is one part of a relationship, most relationships cannot endure if they are based primarily on sexual attraction. In the course of time, many people meet others whom they find more attractive or handsome than the person they married and can become candidates of infidelity if they make decisions not based on will power, but on sexual drive.

Motives for living together before marriage vary from couple to couple. Those who cohabitate primarily for sexual reasons have been found in some studies to have higher divorce rates and more problems with communication and conflict resolution than couples that did not cohabitate before marriage.

Sexuality is a very important and enjoyable aspect of marriage, but it is important that it be integrated into a relationship grounded in love, trust and commitment. While one partner may find another partner very sexy, beautiful or handsome, what else is there about the other partner that he or she appreciates?

What are the qualities you most appreciate in your partner? Does he or she know what you find most attractive about him/her? How often do you compliment your partner? Do your compliments exceed your criticisms by more than five to one? Do you know what your partner finds most attractive about you?

6. I sometimes worry about how my partner's past sexual relationships might have physical or other consequences in our lives.

In light of the existence of various sexually transmitted diseases (STDs), including HIV/AIDS, it is important to know the state of each other's health. The more sex partners a person may have had in the past, the greater potential that person has for being infected with a STD. Appropriate blood tests and cultures can help identify any problems that can, in many cases, be followed up with appropriate treatment.

In addition to physical consequences, a person may also suffer psychological consequences from being intimately involved with another person or other people in the past. If these are genuine concerns, then it is important that they be addressed and resolved as these circumstances can inhibit the ability of maintaining sexual relations between spouses that are essential to a strong marriage.

Do you find yourself often comparing your partner with a past intimate friend or previous spouse in various ways (e.g., emotionally, sexually)? Do you feel that your partner may be comparing you with someone in the past? Are you concerned that your partner might still have some physical or emotional ties with someone he or she may have known that can harm your relationship? Do you still have strong feelings for someone you were close to in the past? Lingering concerns about past relationships should be discussed honestly lest such sentiments harm the foundation of trust upon which a long and loving relationship is built.

7. Our relationship could end if one partner were to be unfaithful.

Most relationships do not survive infidelity particularly in cultures where women enjoy equal rights and enforced legal benefits (e.g., alimony, child support). If a person was unfaithful, was it a singular event for which the unfaithful partner is sincerely sorry? If this is the case, should the guilty person confess this to his or her partner? In singular cases where the guilty partner will never again see the person with whom he or she had sexual relations, most counselors would recommend that the guilty party not raise the issue unless there is a good chance that the other partner may learn of this from someone else. Such a confession could irreparably damage the trust the offended party has for the offender.

In cases where a partner is both emotionally and sexually involved on numerous occasions, potential for discovery and the destruction of the relationship are significantly higher. Like a cancer that needs to be treated by an oncologist, most serious relationship problems need to be addressed by a professional counselor or qualified member of the clergy.

In addition to offering marriage enrichment programs for couples with good relationships who wish to have better ones, some religious groups also offer programs specifically geared toward married couples with serious problems. Unless both partners are eager and willing to benefit from participation in such programs, their effectiveness is limited.

If you had to deal with infidelity in your relationship, would you be more concerned about your partner's emotional or physical involvement with the other individual? Would you be willing to obtain professional help if you were the victim or perpetrator of infidelity? Do you believe that divorce is justified in all cases of infidelity or are there circumstances that might diminish culpability?

8. There are no homosexual feelings on my part or on the part of my partner.

Heterosexuality and homosexuality involve more than simply engaging in sexual actions. A number of reasons have been offered to explain why some people may be homosexuals. Regardless of the position one takes on homosexual orientation and behavior, certain questions need to be considered by dating and engaged individuals if they have any doubts about their heterosexuality.

Are you emotionally more fulfilled when you are with members of your own sex than you are with your heterosexual partner? Were you involved in a homosexual relationship before you started dating your partner? Have you discussed your homosexual experiences, both emotional and physical, with your partner? Serious reservations about one's sexual orientation are best discussed with a professional counselor prior to marriage.

9. I can easily identify at least ten different ways of maintaining intimacy and not losing romance in our relationship.

It's Saturday night and you have a hot date. You're concerned with how you look and plans are in place for what you hope will be a very romantic evening together. You enjoy an intimate candlelight dinner with soft background music and more than just superficial conversation. You feel like you've never been happier in your entire life. The interior feelings that each of you have for one another grow and in time are externalized in a memorable and joyous wedding celebration in the presence of family and friends.

Years later it's Saturday and you and your spouse find yourselves very tired after a long week. The kids around which your lives seem to evolve place great demands on each of you. Will this Saturday night simply be a time to recharge your batteries or can it be an opportunity to reawaken many of the feelings of love and romance that predated your marriage?

What can couples do to help maintain romance in their lives? Here are some romantic weekend suggestions that may prove helpful: Send the kids away to their grandparents, relatives or friends so you can be alone together at least from Saturday to Sunday afternoon. Make reservations for dinner at an upscale restaurant where you can both dress up and have a quiet, intimate dinner together. Go for a romantic walk together, preferably in a scenic area where, in addition to holding hands, you can also sit and chat about the "good times" you've shared over the years. Get a romantic movie, perhaps one that dates back to when you were dating or one that has always had special meaning in your lives. If you don't spend Saturday night in a cozy bed and breakfast or hotel, use candles, flowers and soft music to create a very romantic atmosphere in your home throughout the weekend.

Have you ever given your partner a spontaneous kiss in public? Have you ever hidden a love note to be discovered or sent your partner a card apart from his or her birthday or Valentine's Day? Have you ever called your partner at work or at home and said, "I just called to say 'I love you'?" If getting away for romantic dinners together prove too difficult to arrange or too costly, have you ever considered luncheon encounters? Have you ever thought about how good kids must feel to see their parents kissing? What are some of your own ideas for not losing the spark that ignited your love for one another?

10. I am very well informed of various physical and psychological problems that can affect a decrease in a person's sex drive.

A husband whose wife no longer seemed to be interested in having sex began to question whether his wife still loved him, or whether he may not have been a good lover. It was only after he spoke with his wife's doctor that he came to understand what was really going on in his wife's life. Because most cases of sexual dysfunction are treatable, it's important to share your concerns with your partner and your doctor.

People can suffer from certain physical and psychological sexual problems that reduce their desire or ability to engage in sexual relations. Some of these problems include: lack of sexual interest; inability to become aroused; pain during intercourse; failure to achieve orgasm; erectile dysfunction; premature, inhibited or retrograde ejaculation.

There are a number of causes for sexual disorders in both men and women. Included among some of the causes that impact one's desire or ability to engage in sexual relations are: pregnancy and childbirth, testosterone levels, hormonal imbalances, chronic diseases, alcoholism and drug abuse, marital or relationship problems, stress, depression, fatigue, and past sexual abuse.

The success of treatment for sexual problems depends to a large extent on their underlying causes. The outlook is good for problems related to a treatable physical condition. Psychological problems related to stress, depression, fear or anxiety often can be successfully treated with counseling and improved communication between partners.

If you experienced sexual problems in your relationship, would you and your partner be comfortable in discussing this together or consulting a doctor or therapist? Are you or your partner currently suffering from any physical or psychological problems or engaged in any addictions that can contribute to sexual dysfunction?

TODDLER STRATEGIES

People come from many different family backgrounds -- large families, small families, healthy families and even broken families. From these backgrounds often arise ideas of how people envision the home they are about to build. Couples need to discuss their family vision and their respective responsibilities in regard to having and raising children.

---

1. We are in complete agreement about our desire to have (more) children.

Ordinarily, for a marriage to succeed, the partners must agree upon major issues (e.g., permanency, fidelity, children). If one partner wants to be a mother or father, and the other partner only wants to be a husband or wife, giving in to having or not having children may pose serious problems for the compromised partner. A person's maternal and paternal instincts must not be discounted lightly. How might a partner who gives up having children handle later meeting an attractive unattached person of similar age and background who would deeply like to have children?

Motives for not wanting to have children vary. While some people may be motivated by selfishness, self-centeredness, materialism or careerism, others may have genuine fears based upon other unselfish factors. Many people do not change their feelings about children. There are cases, however, where some partners were initially hesitant to have children but later changed their minds and very much enjoyed being parents.

Some partners who are reluctant to have children have been known to entrust the other partner with most of the responsibilities associated with raising them. This is unfair to the other partner and the children, and may result in behavioral and emotional problems for the child.

By recognizing the unifying effect children can have on a relationship, a partner who does not wish to have children must weigh how this decision may affect their married lives together. Partners may wish to discuss what they might do if they later discover that one or both of them is incapable of having children.

If one or both of you are hesitant to have children, what are the main reasons? Have you thoroughly discussed these reasons? Has the partner who wants children considered breaking off the relationship unless the other partner changes his/her mind about having children?

2. We are not in total agreement about the size of family we would like to have.

One person may have been raised in a large family while the other partner may have been an only child. Such experiences can affect their own attitudes toward family size.

Some people let economic or career factors play a role in determining how many children they may wish to raise. Physical, economic and other circumstances may develop that contribute to a couple's attitude toward children. Some people consider the age of their partner as a determinant for starting a family.

Disagreement between partners over family size can provide an opportunity to discern personal motivations, fears and priorities in their relationship. In the course of reconciling differences in opinion, serious consideration should be given to the meaning of children in marriage. In the midst of this decision-making, thought should also be given to the unifying influence that children can have on a couple's love, as well as the fact that many couples are unable to have children.

Studies show that biological children ordinarily enhance the parent's love for one another. Children from a previous relationship, however, can pose challenges to the bonding of the couple due to the involvement of others (e.g., ex-spouse, ex-love). Finances can also be strained if a partner is required to pay child support as a result of a previous relationship.

What are the real reasons that each partner has for wanting a particular family size? If there are differences in opinion, can a compromise be achieved?

3. We disagree about when we would like to have (more) children.

People who marry when they are in their early 20s often have the option of having children early or waiting until they are older. In light of biological clocks, women who marry in their 30s don't have as much flexibility. Some couples would like to have children when they are young so they can be free of the responsibility of parenthood when they are in their 40s and 50s. Other couples choose to be free of parenting responsibilities in their 20s in order to pursue career goals, travel etc. Children can place a financial strain on a marriage relationship, and some couples choose to wait until they are more financially secure before becoming parents. Many couples discover, however, that they will never be completely financially secure and that there is no perfect time to have children.

Are a person's reasons valid for waiting to have children later rather than earlier? If one partner feels that they are waiting too long, that partner could find his or her love diminishing for the other spouse. How might one or both partners react if they delayed having children only later to discover that they were incapable of having children?

Couples who cannot conceive children through sexual relations may discuss other alternatives (e.g., adoption, infertility treatment). While artificial insemination by the husband (AIH) can result in a child that is the genetic product of the mother and father, artificial insemination by a donor (AID) can in some cases prove problematic if the infertile partner has reservations about raising a child that is the genetic product of an anonymous individual. Some sterile husbands have found it easier to grow attached to a child that their wives have conceived through AID if the child bears even the slightest resemblance to them.

In an effort to avoid conception, some couples employ natural family planning (NFP) methods that identify the fertile period of a woman's menstrual cycle. However, NFP can also be used to help women conceive when this has proven difficult. NFP methods (e.g., ovulation method, sympto-thermal method and the lactation amenorrhea method) should not be confused with calendar rhythm that is a very ineffective family planning method.

Would you and your partner consider the services provided by a fertility clinic if you discovered you were incapable of having children through sexual relations? Are there religious or other reasons one or both of you might have for not using a particular family planning method either to conceive or prevent the conception of a child? Would you consider leaving your partner if he or she put off having children until it was too late?

4. We are in agreement about methods of family planning.

A number of family-planning methods are available today that vary in their degree of effectiveness and safety. Some religious groups, as well as some doctors, have reservations about employing certain family-planning methods on medical or moral grounds. Even if a particular method is physically safer than others, a couple must still consider the motive for delaying or limiting their number of children. A safe method employed for selfish reasons can still have a negative impact on a couple's love relationship. Regardless of what method a couple decides to employ, both partners need to become involved in the decision while constantly reevaluating the issue as circumstances develop and change in their lives.

Are you familiar with the medically documented risks associated with various forms of contraception? Are you in agreement about using certain family planning methods? Which ones would you consider using in an effort to prevent child birth or to help conceive a child?

5. We are in agreement about how we will raise and discipline our children.

It has been said, "Having children is one thing. Raising them is another." The way we raise our children is, to an extent, conditioned on how we ourselves were raised. While we may be inclined to imitate what we may consider to be effective and helpful aspects of our childhood and adolescence, we may also tend to avoid those aspects that we found wanting.

Were we disciplined physically (spanked), or did our parents avoid all forms of physical punishment? Were we expected to help with the household chores and get part-time jobs to help earn spending money, or were we raised in affluence with minor responsibilities? Were there major differences between the ways each partner was raised? Have the partners discussed the importance of avoiding disagreements in the presence of their children, particularly in regard to what their children may or may not do?

In the process of maintaining discipline in the home, it is important that partners are supportive of each other in front of their children. Differences of opinion regarding discipline should be discussed privately between parents. Playing the "mommy against daddy game" to get their way only works if the parents are inconsistent and allow their children to manipulate them.

Raising children is both a challenging and rewarding responsibility. Mistakes are made that are sometimes corrected if and when the parents have other children. Parents should not be too harsh and demanding. At the same time, they should avoid spoiling their children, which can only make it difficult for them to develop and succeed in life.

Do you agree about spanking as an acceptable or unacceptable form of punishment? Have you discussed your respective home experiences in regard to being disciplined? How might you discipline your children differently from the way you were raised?

6. We have different views on adopting children.

Some couples are incapable of having children. Adoption, particularly if a couple meets a number of criteria associated with being potentially good parents, can provide an alternative to having biological children. If a couple knows they are incapable of having children on their own, they would be wise to discuss their attitudes toward adoption before marriage.

Various types of adoption exist that involve children born both in the United States and in other countries. A couple should research regulations that apply to their own qualifications that can affect their eligibility.

Some partners may be concerned about the medical history of an adopted child. While there is some uncertainty in not knowing the complete medical background of an adopted child, particularly those from foreign countries, there are also medical uncertainties involved in having biological children of one's own. There are no medical guarantees when it comes to having either biological or adopted children.

There are also some partners who may be hesitant to adopt children due to a preoccupation with passing on their own genes. Unfortunately, such partners may not prove to be good parents due to the fact that the issue at hand is more about family than it is about genes.

Is your partner open to adopting children? If your partner has reservations about adoption, what is the basis for these reservations? Does the couple have the financial resources not only to adopt a child, but also to raise the child? Are the ages of the couple and the stability of the parents' relationship such that an adoption agency would be eager to support their request to adopt?

7. We differ in our views on abortion.

If a woman becomes pregnant and either she or her partner proposes having an abortion, how will this impact their relationship, particularly if one partner is opposed to abortion? Partners may differ politically or religiously about abortion in general, but how do they view it in relation to their own lives? Are there certain circumstances in which one or both partners feel that an abortion may be justified?

Attitudes about when human life begins and when it may end can affect a couple's relationship far more than their political or religious affiliations. How might they handle a situation involving a pregnant teenage daughter? If one partner had an abortion or participated in an abortion in a past relationship, might that affect their relationship in some way?

Abortion can be a controversial and uncomfortable topic to discuss. However, given the physical and psychological effects it can have in the lives of a couple, it is one issue that needs to be addressed.

How similar or different are your views on abortion? Does you partner know if you had an abortion or helped someone have one in the past? Have you ever demonstrated outside an abortion clinic or attempted to discourage women from having abortions? Have your views on abortion changed over time?

8. We know how to help children cope with the separation of a parent (e.g., deployments).

Children react differently if a parent is required to travel extensively depending on their age, personality and how often a parent may have been gone in the past. Some children mistakenly feel they are responsible for the departure of a parent. Teens sometimes view one parent's absence as an opportunity to be free of a certain degree of discipline. While some children become very concerned about the safety of a traveling parent, other children assume that nothing bad can happen and mom or dad will return without incident.

When a parent is going to leave home for an extended period of time, children should be told exactly what is happening. Children need to know that the departure has nothing to do with them or the other parent. Parents who are deployed for long periods need to tell their children that they are very much loved, even from thousands of miles away. Creative ways can be employed to keep the separated parent close to his/her children (e.g., tape record reading children's books that the other parent will play at bedtime).

One parent discovered the importance of writing each of his children individually when he was away for extended periods. It was only later when his children were grown up that they told him how they felt "special" as a result of those individual communications.

When a partner goes away for a lengthy period of time (e.g., 6-12 month deployment), both spouses and children undergo changes. Hopefully, during the reunion period, the family will adjust to those changes and be renewed in their love for one another. In order to facilitate the reunification process, the returning spouse should not attempt to reassert his or her authority too quickly (e.g., "Now that I'm back, you are no longer going to…"). Such behavior could be perceived as criticism of the partner who "held down the fort" in the absence of the other spouse. The returning partner would be wise to reintegrate himself/herself slowly into the household, to spend quality one-on-one time with the children, and to get away for at least a day or two alone with one's spouse.

What is the longest period of time you have been separated from one another since you started dating or were married? Are you familiar with various resources that help children cope with being separated from a parent?

9. I am familiar with the positive and negative effects children can have upon a couple's relationship.

When two partners give birth to their own children, their love for one another is often strengthened. When a couple marries and one or both of them bring with them a child or children from another relationship, these children can, in some cases, contribute to the dissolution of the marriage. The chances for a marriage to survive involving children from a previous relationship are significantly enhanced when the children are accepting of their stepmother or stepfather.

It is generally more difficult to raise someone else's children than to raise one's own. While it can be difficult in cases where a parent may have died and the other parent remarried, it is even more difficult if one's parents are divorced. A number of factors can make this situation more or less difficult to handle. For example, how does the mother of the children relate to her former husband's new wife? Do the children look upon their father's/mother's new spouse as someone who contributed to their parents' divorce, or are they happy that their mother or father has found a new mate to share life and love? Do the children sometimes try to play a parent against a stepparent when the stepparent may attempt to exercise a certain degree of discipline?

The younger the children are when their parent's remarry, the easier it often is to accept a stepparent into their lives. Teenage children are often more traumatized than young children by divorce. Hence, partners should be well informed of ways to help a child or children avoid experiencing various problems that can result when their parents' divorce.

Unless a couple is too old to have children of their own after one or both of them had children earlier, new born children can not only strengthen the love of the natural parents, but their presence at times can also help their stepbrother(s) and/or stepsister(s) be less critical of their own mother's or father's new spouse.

Because of the challenges that one partner can experience in raising a child or children from the other partner's previous relationship, it is important that a couple thoroughly discuss how they are going to handle this situation. Children may also need to be counseled about how they should relate to a new stepparent in a way so as not to harm their natural parent's chances for love and happiness.

If one or both of you have a child or children from a previous relationship, who has custody and where will they live? Would a stepparent consider adopting the other spouse's children and curtail receiving child support payments if it could strengthen his or her relationship with them? If both partners have children from previous relationships, how well do one partner's children get along with the other partner's children? Have you discussed how one partner might discipline children from the other spouse's previous relationship?

IN-LAWS, OUTLAWS AND OTHERS

Our relationship with our families and friends changes in some ways once we are married. While husbands and wives need to be best friends, they also need good friends and family members to support them throughout their married lives.

---

1. Both of our families are supportive of our relationship.

Family support can be a critical factor in achieving a long-lasting and happy marriage. There are a variety of reasons why some family members and friends may not be supportive of a couple's relationship. Some reasons may be justified, while others may be totally unwarranted.

Some parents and in-laws are very supportive and helpful, while others may be quite the opposite. It is best that issues such as visits over the holidays and contact with grandchildren be addressed by a son or daughter rather than by a son-in-law or daughter-in-law.

While it is generally a good sign when family and friends approve of our relationship, why might some people question it? Are there ulterior motives associated with some people's lack of support (e.g., possessive parent or close friend)? Are there valid reasons for concern on the part of our loved ones (e.g., bad habits, problematic behavior)? Valid concerns need to be examined and discussed by the couple. Unwarranted objections are best dismissed.

2. My partner's family at times becomes too involved in our relationship.

After a woman had a long-distance conversation with her parents, her partner said, "You're always on the phone with your folks. Tell me one thing. Do you love me or your parents?" Such a question is unfair. She loves both her parents and her partner. What is important is that she is able to communicate her love to them both without one or the other feeling slighted. Partners who enjoy a good relationship with their parents will often develop a similar relationship with their own children.

If couples strive to maintain a healthy balance between their love for one another and their respective families of origin, so, too, must their parents neither become too involved in their lives nor be so distant that their children fail to feel their love and support. If one partner feels that the other's mother or father may be interfering in their relationship, such concern must be expressed in a sensitive way so as not to create major "in-law" problems. When the feelings of one partner's parents are offended or hurt, it can harm the couple's relationship with the offended parents, the relationship between the two partners and the relationship between grandchildren and grandparents.

Diplomacy is key in maintaining a healthy balance in the way each partner relates to his or her parents and in-laws. A couple and their children need the love and support of their parents and grandparents just as much as the couple's parents need the love of their children and grandchildren. Just as no one person is an island, so too no couple is an island. All couples need the support of relatives and friends.

Do either or both of your families interfere too much in your lives? If one or both of your families are not supportive of your relationship, what is the basis for their lack of support? Can other family members or friends help to remedy this situation?

3. I am uncomfortable with some of my partner's friends.

The friends we make say a lot about who we really are. Even though opposites may attract and their differences may complement each other, people tend to gravitate to others who share common interests and values. While one person may not like all of the other partner's friends, ordinarily, partners who share a lot in common likewise enjoy sharing the friends that each partner has made over time. If one partner has a number of friends with whom the other partner feels uncomfortable or unaccepted, the couple may have to examine what it is that separates the one partner from the other partner's friends.

Do your friends support your relationship with your partner? Are your friends optimistic about your potential for a life-long, loving and happy marriage? What are the values you find important in your friends? Are there specific reasons you might find yourself uncomfortable with some of your partner's friends? Are they smokers or drug abusers? Do they use foul language? Are your partner's friends dangerous, abusive or just different?

4. I am concerned about the degree of my partner's involvement with some of his/her friends.

Some couples believe that once they get married, they can stop seeing their old friends. Such thinking can have harmful consequences because friendships are valuable and help mold who we are.

Involvement with people other than one's partner should complement one's relationship. Going out with "the boys" or "the girls" occasionally can prove to be a healthy diversion and provide an opportunity for "male bonding" or "female bonding." It is only when such "bonding" distracts from the bond that unite a couple that one may have to reexamine how much time and energy one may be investing in outside activities and associations. Partners should cultivate relationships that can invigorate and sustain their most treasured relationship in life.

Would you mind if your partner kept in touch with an ex-spouse or people from the past that he or she dated? Are there any individuals with whom you would like your partner to disassociate? Are there any people or couples with whom you would like you and your partner to become better associated?

5. I am hesitant to share with my partner some emotional hurts I experienced in my life (e.g., abuse, broken relationships).

A husband could not understand why his wife was not responsive to his sexual advances. He went to the gym to become more muscular and even read various books about what women enjoyed when it came to lovemaking. When he continued to be unsuccessful in arousing his wife, he suggested that they meet with a counselor. In the course of the counseling, the counselor learned that the woman was sexually abused at home when she was young. Once the counselor was able to help the wife distinguish between her abuser and her husband, their love life, as well as their entire married life, improved significantly.

By discussing past emotional hurts, some couples are able more effectively to address problems that may be affecting their relationship. Some couples discover that they are not able to resolve these problems on their own and may require professional counseling.

Partners should also share with one another significant positive emotional events that have occurred in their lives. Knowledge of these events can only help them understand and love each other all the more.

Can you identify emotional hurts that your partner experienced in his/her life? Is your partner sensitive to any emotional scars you may have from the past? What positive emotional experiences and accomplishments have helped promote your partner's sense of self-worth?

6. My partner is very sensitive to any relational or emotional problems I may have experienced in the past.

We all come to a relationship with good and bad experiences. For example, if a partner was involved in a previous relationship that ended as a result of infidelity, that partner may find that he or she might be particularly sensitive about always accounting for the other partner's presence. After being hurt once, we tend to become sensitive about being hurt a second time. It is important that we do not transfer the shortcomings of a person from a past relationship to our current partner who is a different person altogether from someone in the past.

Is your partner aware of any relational or emotional problems you may have experienced in the past? Are you hesitant to share these experiences with your partner? Some people who share emotional hurts sometimes discover that their partners are far more understanding than they imagined.

7. We both have made a number of good friends and have similar and complementary interests.

Even though we enjoy our partner's company, we might like to see our partner pursue certain interests or friendships that can complement our own relationship and afford us a certain amount of breathing space and freedom. Partners, particularly those who find themselves left behind when their mates are away on business, need to be engaged in healthy pursuits that can contribute to their own growth while preventing them from engaging in activities that can harm their relationship.

Most military bases and civilian communities welcome volunteers to assist organizations like the Red Cross in meeting a variety of needs. Involvement in such organizations allows partners to find fulfillment in the contributions they provide and to make new friends in the process. Healthy friendships and interests outside of a marital relationship can serve to make a couple only closer and stronger in their love for one another.

What common activities do you enjoy doing together? What activity (e.g., sport) would you like to learn that your partner already has mastered? Are there any base, civic, sporting or church activities that you wish you could engage in together?

8. We have a healthy balance between the time we spend together, the time we spend alone, and the time we spend with family and friends.

Each of us appreciates some quiet time in our lives. Once in a while, it is good for us to be alone, to meditate and to reflect upon where we are coming from, where we are now and where we hope to go with our lives. While we enjoy being with our loved ones, we also appreciated being afforded some "space" from time to time.

As children enter the picture, it can become harder to find some quiet time. Consequently, it is important that partners plan time for themselves both as a couple and as individuals. Time away from the kids can involve a late night dinner on a Friday or Saturday night when the children are asleep; a romantic walk in a scenic place; or even a bath complete with candles and champagne.

In addition to setting time aside for oneself and time apart from the children, partners also need to spend time with friends and relatives whose love and support can enrich their marital relationship. We all need others whose lives can help and challenge us to constantly grow in a variety of ways.

Moving from duty station to duty station challenges military couples to make new friends while keeping in touch with good friends made at previous commands. Many couples have found that an overseas tour in a foreign culture can afford the opportunity of bonding not only with other Americans, but also with foreign nationals. Children from military families likewise benefit and mature faster than children from civilian families as a result of their exposure to a broader variety of people from around the United States and the world.

Do you and your partner have common interests that afford you opportunities to relax together (e.g., sports, travel)? Do you find yourself either neglected or too possessed by your partner? Does your partner afford you enough space and opportunities to pursue your own interests? Have you tried to teach each other skills you each possess that can enhance your togetherness? Do you have relatives and friends whom you can visit and whose own marriages can inspire and strengthen your own relationship?

9. Some people questioned that we - may be marrying / married – too soon.

An analogy can be drawn between marriage and pregnancy. Timing is a critical factor in regard to pregnancy. If a woman gives birth prematurely, the child may not survive. Had the child stayed in the womb for nine months, instead of only three, the baby could have survived and have enjoyed a long-life.

Timing is likewise critical in regard to marriage. If a couple marries too soon, before their relationship matures to a point where they are truly ready to commit themselves to each other for life, they may later find themselves unhappily married or divorced, instead of enjoying a long-life of happiness together. On the other hand, a partner who is afraid to make a commitment, and continually finds excuses as to why the "m" word should not be raised, may likewise be jeopardizing the long-term future of the relationship.

There are a number of reasons military personnel tend to marry much younger than their civilian counterparts. While service men and women can develop close bonds of friendship, they can also experience deep loneliness particularly if they are stationed thousands of miles away from family and hometown friends. While all people experience loneliness to some degrees, escaping from it should not be the primary reason for getting married.

Another reason a number of young military personnel marry stems from their belief that they will make more money and live more comfortably than if they remained single. Increased pay and family entitlements over the years have contributed to this perception. With the birth of a child, however, couples come to realize that they had more money to spend when they were single than when they are now married.

When military personnel return to their hometowns following basic training or after completing training in a particular field, their reunions with girl friends or boy friends may result in someone getting pregnant. Unfortunately, most marriages involving pregnant teenagers end in divorce. The potential for divorce is lowered in cases involving pregnancy when marriage plans were discussed prior to discovery.

Rather than marrying while the woman is pregnant, couples may wish to consider getting married after the child is born. It is an encouraging sign if the relationship continues to grow stronger after the child is born. However, if the birth of the child proves to weaken the couple's relationship and they find themselves less united after the birth, they may find that it was wise that they did not marry during the pregnancy.

If the couple decides not to marry following the birth of the child, it is important that the mother files for child support while she still has contact with the father. Unofficial financial support agreements are often broken once the partner providing support becomes involved in another relationship.

One additional reason that some military couples marry too early is because of financial costs associated with moving one partner's furniture. If the marriage takes place before the military member receives orders to his or her next duty station, the government will pay to move both partners' household goods. However, if the military member receives orders before the marriage is contracted, the government will only pay to move the military member's effects, thus requiring the military member to pay for the other partner's move at his or her own expense.

Some relatives and friends are sometimes able to see more clearly than the couple themselves what may be going on in a particular relationship. What are the impressions the people close to you have about your relationship?

The reasons people have for getting married vary from selfish and superficial ones to reasons that are profound and very loving. Ordinarily, people marry for more than simply one reason. What are your real reasons for wanting to marry? If you are already married, are the reasons you have for staying married different from the ones you had for getting married? Can you see yourself happily married five, ten, or twenty years from now?

10. We have discussed the possibility of a parent living with us if the need were to arise.

When a parent is a widow or widower, circumstances may develop wherein he or she should no longer live alone. While some parents may prefer moving to a retirement home rather than moving in with one of their children, financial and other conditions may exist that preclude such a move.

If the physical condition of one of your parent's were to require full-time nursing care, would he or she be able to assume the high costs involved in moving into a nursing home? Would you be willing to have a parent live with you if the need arose? The way a couple cares for their parents is often the way their own children will treat them when they are older.

GREAT EXPECTATIONS

Past performance is often an indicator of future behavior. Recognizing that people are not changed by a wedding ceremony, partners need to honestly discuss their likes and dislikes in the present, as well as their hopes and dreams for the future.

---

1. I wish I knew more about my partner's past so I don't have to worry about how my partner might act in the future.

It takes a certain amount of time for people to get to know one another well enough to make a life-long commitment to each other. Most American couples know each other for at least a year before they marry. The less we know about someone, the greater potential there is to be surprised after we are married.

Because most people are not aware of their shortcomings as much as others recognize them, it cannot hurt to ask one's partner, "What do I say or do at times that you would like me to change?" Some partners might point to bad habits that they would like their partners to discontinue, while others might suggest that their partners put into practice certain actions they may find lacking. For example, a partner might suggest, "I'd like you to spend less time on the computer" or "I wish you would be more helpful with the household chores." Unless partners are interested in making improvements in their lives, and unless they are willing to articulate their respective expectations, their relationships might be deprived of growth that otherwise could occur.

Past performance is often an indicator of future behavior. While we can change, we can only change to a certain degree. Are there certain problematic actions on the part of your partner rooted in the past that you would like to see changed? Have you discussed these matters with your partner? How do you feel these actions may be harming your relationship? Can these problems be solved between yourselves or do you believe that professional help is in order? See how your partner might respond to the question, "What can I do to exceed your expectations?"

2. My partner and I are in agreement about leaving or staying on active duty, and we have discussed what we might do after we leave military service.

A number of couples enjoy military life with the opportunity of living in a variety of countries around the world, along with other benefits (e.g., housing, medical) that vary in quality from place to place and service to service. Other couples may find themselves longing to be closer to their own families, as well as their families of origin. Some couples are fearful that that they may be drawn apart as a result of multiple periods of separation that contribute to a high divorce rate among military couples. Others marry with the intent of staying in the military, only later to change their minds for a variety of reasons.

Circumstances can occur where one may be required to leave the military involuntarily (e.g., as the result of a pass-over for promotion or a disciplinary or medical problem). If this occurs, does the couple know how they will support themselves as civilians?

Military couples approaching retirement need to discuss where they plan to live and what they intend to do. The proximity of one's children, siblings or parents often influences this decision. The military offers classes designed to assist retiring personnel make a smooth transition from military to civilian life. One cannot emphasize enough the importance of attending such classes.

What steps might you begin to take while you are still in the military to prepare for life in the civilian sector (e.g., academic studies that might prepare you for civilian employment)? Would you be willing to move to advance your spouse's career? Are you aware of the importance of job satisfaction and how it can affect a marriage relationship?

3. I am satisfied with how we have decided to divide our various household tasks (e.g., cooking, cleaning, paying the bills).

Each couple must decide who is most interested and able to carry out certain household tasks without burdening a particular member with a disproportionate amount of the workload. While one partner may undertake some tasks, the other mate may perform other chores. And still both partners may share other responsibilities. Circumstances may develop wherein the division of labor may be altered. For example, if neither partner has any interest in cooking, eating out often may prove too costly, thereby moving one partner to develop certain culinary skills.

What might be traditional roles of husbands and wives in certain cultures may have to be negotiated when partners from two different cultures marry. Tensions can arise if one partner feels that he or she has a disproportionate number of household responsibilities. For example, if only one partner is fully employed, is he or she also expected to cook, clean, sew and pay the bills? At the same time, if only one spouse is fully employed, does he or she feel the other partner is responsible for all the household tasks?

Many couples will sit down and develop a list of chores based upon what each of them likes and dislikes to do. Tasks that both of them dislike may be shared or performed by someone else. For example, if both spouses disliked cleaning the bathrooms and the kitchen, they may contract with a maid or cleaning service to have this task completed for them.

Certain circumstances may arise where one might get behind in one's tasks. It's important to be able to distinguish between one getting behind in one's chores verses procrastinating on a regular basis. In cases where certain chores do not seem to be getting done in a timely manner, it may be wise to consider renegotiating that particular responsibility.

Did you both grow up in homes that had similar levels of cleanliness and orderliness? How orderly were your quarters after each of you left home? Have you decided how you will share household responsibilities? Are you comfortable with your division of labor? Do you both recognize and agree that chores are a shared responsibility?

4. We have discussed and we are in agreement about the issue of both partners working.

In today's economy, most young husbands and wives are both employed. Employment opportunities in large urban areas often allow both partners to work better than in some rural or overseas locations.

Dual employment on the part of both partners is a question that needs to be addressed, particularly when the couple has small children. The availability of child care can often be a factor in determining whether a spouse will work outside the home. Some spouses decide to cease working as long as there are preschool children at home. Partners who have full-time jobs need to discuss how they can successfully raise children and still pursue their respective careers. Couples with children should not base their decision about dual employment solely on the financial gains that can be achieved when both partners are employed.

Are you in agreement about whether one spouse should stay at home and raise the children or if that spouse should continue to hold down a job? Have you discussed your feelings about one partner going unaccompanied to a new duty station while the other partner remains behind and employed in his/her current location?

5. We have never had any arguments about – wedding plans / getting a divorce.

It's been said, "A wedding is a day. A marriage is a lifetime." While such a statement points to the importance of preparing for married life more than for the wedding day itself, most couples invest considerable time and money into planning a wedding that will be truly memorable for themselves, their families and their friends. The way a couple handles planning the many details surrounding a wedding offers some insight into how they might handle future major undertakings. It is important that the couple keep the events of the day in perspective. The photographs and video will be shelved in time, and, chances are, no one will ever remember what food was served at the reception.

Are those involved in planning the wedding willing to compromise or are they intent on always having their own way? Are the partners able to diplomatically handle their parents without hurting their feelings? Instead of taking rigid stands and arguing about relatively minor details, the couple can learn some good lessons early about "the art of compromise."

While dating couples can get into arguments over wedding plans, married couples can at times contemplate getting a divorce. Even though half of the marriages in the United States end in divorce, it is estimated that about half of the marriages that end in divorce could be saved with professional help. Just as a person does not have to die of appendicitis when a surgeon is available to perform an appendectomy, so too can many couples be saved from a painful relationship and a subsequent divorce with the help of a counselor, chaplain or civilian member of the clergy.

If a partner ever raised the issue of divorce, has either partner discussed going for counseling to improve and save the relationship? If a person is smart enough to go to a doctor when certain symptoms become more problematic, why would a couple not seek professional help if they are incapable of resolving their relationship problems that only continue to become more painful? The earlier serious marital problems are addressed, the better the chances are of resolving them in an amicable manner. Counselors at family support centers and chaplains are readily available to help military couples who wish to resolve relationship problems and deepen their love for one another.

6. We are in agreement about what kind of home we would like to have and can afford to buy.

One potentially stressful period in a couple's relationship involves purchasing a home. Some military couples, given the frequent moves they experience in the course of a 20 to 30 year career, may find themselves buying and selling a few homes. If a couple purchases a home with mortgage payments so high that they have difficulty paying their other bills, the financial strain they experience could harm their relationship. On the other hand, if they purchase a home that does not meet their needs, and they find that they could have afforded a better residence, this could also be the source of ongoing dissatisfaction.

Housing costs are generally higher the closer one lives to a large city. Lower housing costs farther from downtown are offset by higher transportation expenses as well as longer and more stressful commuting periods.

While renting may be wiser in an area where property values don't have much potential to increase or where the couple will most likely not settle, purchasing a home may prove to be financially rewarding elsewhere if only as an investment. Whether a couple purchases a home to live in for the rest of their lives or simply as a house they will occupy for a set number of years, the decision should be made by both partners after careful study and deliberation.

Some commands require that married personnel live in base quarters if such housing is available. Have you discussed housing issues and what your preferences might be (e.g., base housing verses living in the civilian community)? Will the location of good schools for your children influence where you may wish to live? Do long and stressful commutes in heavy traffic affect your personality in a way that impacts your relationship with coworkers and loved ones?

7. We cannot seem to agree about our future career plans.

A relationship is capable of enduring only so much change, particularly unexpected change. The more aware a couple is about what may change in the future, the more ready they usually are to accept it. If a military couple marries with the intention of leaving the armed services at the completion of a tour of duty, the transition from military to civilian life is much easier than it would be for a couple who are unexpectedly forced to leave the military. While we cannot predict what will occur, a couple should be prepared to discuss what shape they would like their future to take.

Discussions about the future often involve expectations. Partners who have unrealistic expectations often experience disappointment. If the disappointment grows and the expectations are not reevaluated, this can lead in time to despair and the dissolution of the relationship.

It's wise to identify and discuss one's expectations, as well as to address any disagreements about the future, prior to getting married (e.g., one partner wants to leave the military and fly as a commercial pilot, while the other wants him to leave and join her in the teaching profession). (e.g., one partner wants to leave his or her job and relocate to another part of the country while the other partner wants to remain close to relatives and friends). One should respect and appreciate one's partner's aspirations while acknowledging just how much we are willing to compromise.

Career plans can be affected by the arrival of children. This may not only move the mother to stay at home and care for the kids, but it could also cause the father to assume the role of "Mr. Mom." While there are benefits associated with dads staying home and caring for the children, there are also challenges that may require the couple to reevaluate this arrangement particularly as the children get older.

Are your career expectations for the future realistic and attainable? Are you able to resolve any disagreements about your careers by compromising without feeling that you "won the battle but lost the war?" Would either of you wish to stay at home and raise the children? What would you like your lives to look like in 10, 20 or 30 years from now?

8. Our ages are a concern to some family members and friends.

Some military personnel marry people who are very young, while others marry people who are ten to twenty years older than themselves. While the median age at first marriage in the United States is about 27 for men and 25 for women, military personnel tend to marry much younger. It is not surprising that divorce rates are higher in the military than in the civilian sector.

One problem associated with marrying someone very young is the great potential for change. People change a lot more between 18 and 25 than between 25 and 30. Consequently, a person married at 18 is often a very different person at 25. In these circumstances, it is not unusual to hear, "You're not the same person I married." Additionally, it requires a certain degree of maturity to cope with the challenges of being a military spouse. Multiple long-term separations, frequent moves and limited financial resources are but a few of the formidable tasks that often prove too overwhelming for young military spouses to handle.

Some young male personnel have also been known to marry women much older than themselves. A 20-year-old serviceman who is sexually involved with a 40-year-old woman may not be concerned at this point in his life with their age differences. However, when he is 30 and she is 50, he may be more attracted to women his own age. Consequently, while it is not uncommon for men to marry younger women, few marriages succeed in which a young serviceman marries a considerably older woman.

A service member who plans on marrying someone who is either very young or much older needs to ask what is his or her primary motivation. If the relationship is primarily sexual and influenced by loneliness that young military people experience when they are far from home, the chances for success are extremely low.

One problem associated with younger women marrying older men involves children. Is the man desirous or capable of having children? Does he have children from a previous relationship? If so, does he have custody or provide child-support for these children?

When a marriage does not succeed, not only are there divorce costs to be considered, but there may also be child-support payments. One can expect to pay over $100,000 in child-support payments by the time a child reaches the age at which support is no longer required. How much money could one save if one invested wisely about $500 every month over a period of some 18 years? Could one make about $500,000?

Apart from the money involved in marrying too young, the impact that divorce has on children cannot be measured in dollars and cents. Much pain and anguish could be avoided on the part of husbands, wives and children if partners did not rush one of the most important decisions of their lives.

Are there relatives or friends that would like you to delay getting married at this time? What are the reasons they have for making this recommendation? Have you considered the consequences of getting married only later to divorce as the result of a rushed or premature decision to marry?

9. I have some doubts about - marrying / staying married to - my partner.

It is not unusual to have some second thoughts about getting married. In so far as no relationship is perfect and no two people are compatible in all ways, many people will question their decision to marry both before and after marriage. It is important to distinguish between premarital nervousness and reservations grounded in unresolved differences or shortcomings. Serious concerns about important issues (e.g., children, fidelity, permanence) are a good reason to delay a marriage.

While loneliness, sex and money are factors in every relationship, the issue is to marry the right person for the right reasons. A father once told his son that the way he would know if a woman he was dating was "the one," was by asking himself, "Is this the woman with whom I want to spend the rest of my life?" If the answer is "yes," then one should take steps to ensure that the relationship grows and matures. If one answers "no," however, then one should avoid both leading the other person on and undertaking actions that might cause physical and/or emotional harm.

Whether you are preparing to marry or if you are already married, you need to ask yourself, "Is my partner my best friend?" If the answer to that question is "no," then you really need to take a hard look at your relationship. If you discover that it is superficial, are you willing to take steps to deepen and strengthen it?

Many married people question whether they want to stay married to their spouse, particularly when they are experiencing unresolved and persistent problems. While both men and women go through phases that may tempt them to become involved with someone else, acting on these feelings can be affected by alcohol consumption that can lower one's inhibitions, by the willingness of a third party, and other factors. Rather than risk the dissolution of a loving relationship that may simply need to be revitalized, a dissatisfied partner should communicate his or her feelings as to what he or she finds missing in their relationship. Professional counseling may be needed if the couple is not able to resolve matters on their own.

If one person is hesitant about getting married, he or she should articulate the reasons behind such feelings. Might one partner's reservations be based on one or more shortcomings on the part of the other partner? If so, is the other partner even aware of possible failings on his or her part?

Is your partner your best friend? Are you a much better person because of your partner? Do you take a long-term view of marriage and see yourselves happily married 20-30 years from now?

10. We are well prepared to deal with any number of tragedies in the future.

Sickness, chronic disease and death within a marriage and family can challenge a couple to recognize how deep their love is for one another. These challenging experiences can involve one or both of the partners, their children, as well as their parents.

While most couples look forward to having children, how would you react if your child were born with severe disabilities or died at a young age? Couples who suffer the loss of a child are encouraged to share their feelings with one another. Similar to what can occur in the stages of death and dying, couples that lose a child can experience anger, depression, guilt and a host of other feelings. Unfortunately, sometimes people suppress their feelings or, especially in cases of accidental deaths, they may blame a spouse or other child for not having prevented the accident. There is also a tendency in such circumstances to react by being overprotective of other children in the family. Families who find themselves unable to cope over time with the death of a child should seek professional assistance in dealing with the grieving process.

It has also been said that for a couple to say they are truly happy, they have to experience at least five good times for every one bad time. What ratio of good to bad times do you believe exists in your relationship? Have your number of good times to bad times grown, decreased or remained constant over the course of time?

DIVINE INTERVENTION

Individual and shared religious views can have a major impact upon marriage and family life. Studies show that shared religious practice contributes to higher degrees of marital happiness and reduces the chances of divorce. A couple's spirituality affects not only their own lives but also the lives of their children and those around them.

1. We are in agreement about where - we will marry / we were married – (i.e., in a civil ceremony or in a particular religious service).

Some people question the rationale of getting married in a church, synagogue or mosque without being "practicing" Christians, Jews or Muslims. While some members of the clergy will conduct weddings for people who are not active members of their congregations, many require that one partner be actively involved or registered in their faith group before they will conduct the wedding ceremony.

Unlike a civil marriage that simply grants legal recognition to one's marriage vows, a religious wedding ordinarily reflects one or both partners' membership in a religious community with certain set beliefs and practices (e.g., prayer, fasting, works of charity). If one or both partners are religious individuals, they will ordinarily prefer a religious wedding to a strictly civil wedding. Religious regulations in regard to qualifications, as well as how and where the wedding can take place, differ amongst various faith groups.

Chaplains and civilian clergy can help a couple discern if being married in a religious ceremony is appropriate at this time in their lives. Some couples will marry initially in a civil ceremony and later celebrate their commitment in a religious ceremony when they are more religiously involved.

Is it important to you or your partner that you be married in a religious ceremony? Do you feel pressure from either of your parents to be married by a member of the clergy? Have you met with a chaplain, minister, priest, rabbi or imam to discuss requirements in regard to having one of them conduct your marriage, particularly if you and your partner have been raised in different religious traditions?

2. I understand how a couple's moral and religious values can affect their marital success and happiness.

Are human relationships primarily physical or spiritual in nature? If our relationships with one another were primarily physical and sexual in nature, then good-looking and well-proportioned people would be happy, while unattractive and overweight people would be unhappy in their relationships. If a woman says to her partner, "Don't touch me," it is not because he is not handsome or a good lover. It's ordinarily because he said or did something to hurt or upset her. Once they spiritually become reunited and the emotional gap is repaired that separates them, the woman will again become affectionate in sharing her love for her mate.

Most people acknowledge that it is more fulfilling to make love, involving a spiritual sharing of one's heart and soul, than simply to have sex. It is for this reason that couples who pray together report having better sex than people who do not "exercise spiritually." While being more sexually fulfilled is not the reason most people worship together, many people who pray together appreciate the fact their chances for a happy and life-long marriage are enhanced as a result of their religious practice.

Do you believe that prayer is an important part of family life? Do you believe regular attendance at worship services is important? If you were raised in different religious traditions, what direction do you see yourselves taking that can affect the religious beliefs of any children you might have?

3. We have yet to agree upon the role of religion in our relationship (e.g., attending worship).

There are relationships where both partners are active in the same faith group; where the partners are active in different faith groups; where only one partner is active in a religious body; and where neither partners are religiously involved. If both partners are raised in the same faith, their chances of practicing that particular belief are enhanced. It is ordinarily easier to attend worship as a family when both parents are active members of the same faith group. When one parent attends worship services and the other parent remains at home, the chances of their children practicing the faith of the religious parent as adults are reduced.

Do you plan to attend worship services together, alone or only on rare occasions (e.g., funerals and weddings)? Does your partner have any reservations about your monetary contributions to your faith group? Is either partner interested in converting to the other partner's faith group?

4. We have unresolved questions about the religious upbringing of our children.

Disagreements about the religious upbringing of children occur most frequently among partners who come from very different faith backgrounds. This problem is exacerbated when grandparents object to the religious education their grandchildren may be receiving. Most parents recognize the need for their children to possess values and to develop morally. Most faith groups provide such moral development.

Parents also recognize problems associated with attempting to raise children in two distinct faith traditions. Children with parents who adhere to distinct religious beliefs and practices are generally raised and educated in the faith of one parent, while being taught at home to respect the tenants of the other parent's religion. Ultimately, when children grow up and leave home, it will be their decision to accept or reject whatever religious education and training they may have received at home and at school.

Will you raise your children in a particular faith tradition? If one partner is from a tradition that baptizes infants and the other is from a faith group that waits until adolescence or adulthood to offer baptism, which tradition will be followed? Will your children attend public schools, or would you like them to be enrolled in parochial or private schools?

5. I am satisfied with my partner's attitude toward my religious beliefs and practices.

Some people grow up with good religious experiences (developing a close relationship with a priest, minister, rabbi or imam). Others grow up with bad or unmemorable religious experiences. Still other people grow up with no religious experiences. If partners come from very different faith backgrounds, the potential for religious misunderstanding is greater than for two partners who were raised in the same faith group. For example, if a Christian is dating a non-Christian who mocks a Christmas crèche, such derision could erode, and possibly destroy, the love that brought the couple together.

Were your respective religious experiences growing up positive, negative or nonexistent? Would you be willing to learn more about your partner's religious beliefs and practices? Have you ever disagreed with one another over an interpretation of a particular scripture passage? Do you and your partner have a respectful attitude toward people from different faith groups?

MISCELLANEOUS

Statements in this area address leisure time, public behavior, personal habits, household concerns, foreign relationships and second marriages. While we may accomplish some changes on our own (e.g., stop smoking, go to school, lose weight), certain addictions may require professional help if they are to be arrested (e.g., drug addiction, spousal abuse, alcoholism). The challenges of marrying a foreign national, or being married for a second or third time, might also require special assistance and counseling.

1. I wish my partner spent less time on the computer, watching DVDs or television.

One reason that people marry among others is for companionship. When partners spend an inordinate amount of time in front of a television screen or computer monitor, their human relationships with their spouses and children can suffer. A healthy balance needs to be achieved between one's married life and one's video life. The way we apportion our time is indicative of what is truly important in our lives.

Couples who have been married for many years acknowledge the importance of prioritizing their time together as a couple. Even when children enter into the picture, husbands and wives still need quality time together apart from the kids.

If partners marry because they are best friends, couples also divorce because they have grown apart. By giving priority to time spent together with one's spouse the potential for growing apart is significantly reduced.

If a husband promised to take his wife and children on an outing on Saturday and later learned that his favorite college football team was playing a game that will be televised at that same time, could he record the game and watch it after the outing? Do you feel you're competing with the Internet or the television for your partner's time? Do you ever take time to discuss the news or issues that can strengthen and stimulate your relationship? Are there activities that you can undertake together that can enhance your love and companionship?

2. I have never been embarrassed to be seen with my partner in public.

While it is a very good sign that we enjoy being seen with our partner in public, a relationship can be harmed if one person is embarrassed by the other partner's public behavior or appearance. Most people want to be proud of their partner's looks, intelligence, talents, and sense of humor. When one partner acts in an inappropriate manner (intoxicated or foul-mouthed.), the other partner may become hesitant to go out in public with him or her.

Are you sometimes disturbed by your partner's sense of humor? What actions might you find embarrassing on the part of your partner? Can he or she restrain this behavior? If the other partner is unwilling or incapable of correcting these problems, are you willing to accept this behavior throughout your married life?

3. We agree about how neat and clean our home should be kept.

Some partners grow up in very neat and clean homes, while others may have been raised in homes that were somewhat disorderly. If someone is dating a person whose apartment is very cluttered, can one expect that a messy apartment today might be replaced by a very untidy home tomorrow? The presence of small children will make maintaining an ordered home all the more difficult to achieve. While a person need not be fanatical about everything being in perfect order, both partners should agree upon a level of orderliness and cleanliness. Sharing household responsibilities can enhance chances for a well kept home.

Do you have similar levels of household cleanliness? Have you discussed sharing certain household tasks (cleaning the bathrooms, vacuuming and mopping the floors, doing the dishes, washing the clothes)? If neither partner is intent upon doing housework, can you afford to pay for a house cleaning service?

4. I am concerned about some of my partner's habits.

Some people are able to arrest certain habits in the course of their lives, while other people continue to engage in destructive or annoying behaviors until the day they die. It is unrealistic to believe that a person will necessarily change for the better after the wedding.

A partner may do things that are far more upsetting than he or she may realize. For example, if you perceive that your partner raises his or her eyes upward as a way of criticizing something you may have said or done, you need to address how this action makes you feel. He or she may not fully appreciate how insulting and hurtful this action may be perceived. By using "I" statements (instead of accusatory "you" statements) to explain how you are upset by such sarcastic actions, your chances of curtailing such acts are increased. Partners need to discuss habitual and addictive behaviors and decide what course of action to take in order to curtail particularly harmful habits.

A person's bad habits can prove to be the source of embarrassment for one's partner. This can include such actions as becoming intoxicated, passing gas, making derogatory remarks about one's partner, or monopolizing the conversation. Bad habits that can be very annoying at home can include leaving clothes or towels on the floor, leaving the toilet seat in the up position or failing to replace an empty roll of toilet paper.

While most people cannot identify certain things they do that their partner's may find offensive, their partners, on the other hand, can readily identify these shortcomings. What would you like your partner to refrain from doing that you feel would enhance your relationship? Are there any habits you feel might threaten the stability and happiness of your relationship? Does your partner need help (e.g., Alcoholics Anonymous) in arresting certain self-destructive behaviors?

5. We are in agreement about the presence of pets around the house.

There are both benefits and problems associated with having pets. Some studies show that pets can help reduce stress and loneliness. They can also have a positive impact on relationships particularly when both partners are involved in caring for the pet. It is not at all uncommon for young married couples to have pets as a prelude to having children.

In some cases pets have also contributed to marital discord, even divorce. Arguments surrounding their care, expense, cleanliness, and the travel limitations they can place on couples, have moved some partners to say, "Either the pet goes, or I go."

Some people enjoy pets more than others. A partner who grew up with a pet may be inclined to want one as an adult. Also, couples that do not or cannot have children are often inclined to have pets.

A number of couples find that their work schedules make caring for a pet too demanding and restrictive. While pets can provide companionship and some can even provide protection, they also can also require a high degree of maintenance and limit a couple's housing options in certain locations.

Some children ask their parents to allow them to have a pet. If parents acquiesce to their wishes, will the children walk the dog or help clean the fish tank? If a family acquires a cat, who will look after it when they are out of town?

Before a couple acquires a pet for themselves or their children, they need to weigh the positive and negative reasons associated with having it and reach a joint decision in this regard. Couples should never even think of acquiring a pet without achieving consensus on this potentially divisive matter.

Have you discussed the pros and cons involved in having pets? Have you talked about having a particular kind of pet? Will one or both partners be responsible for caring for the pet?

6. I wish my partner were more attentive in remembering special occasions and acknowledging them in special ways (e.g., cards, flowers, gifts).

Some people are more organized than others are in remembering special occasions. Economic background and family of origin experiences might also influence how generous and giving a person might be in regard to gift giving. If some people have not been too attentive in remembering special occasions or very generous in acknowledging those occasions, it does not mean that they cannot show improvement in these areas. Failure to remember important occasions such as birthdays and anniversaries with a meaningful (not necessarily expensive) gift can result in a partner feeling unloved or unappreciated.

If one partner tells another partner not to get him or her a birthday present, should one be surprised if a present is not forthcoming? Could this be a problem of communication or interpretation? When a person says, "I don't need anything," he or she may actually be saying, "Don't ask me what I want — just surprise me!"

Roses are symbols of passion and love. Even if the price of a dozen long stemmed roses is particularly high in your area, consider the impact that one rose can make.

What can you do to help your partner be more organized in remembering special occasions? Do you find your partner generous when it comes to giving you gifts? Have you communicated to your partner what you particularly appreciate (e.g., jewelry, music, books)? What personalized gift can you give your partner that would make him/her happy?

7. We were both born in the Unite States.

Overseas tours of duty and deployments bring U.S. military personnel into contact with men and women from a variety of countries. Some of these contacts lead to dating relationships and marriage. While a number of U.S. military personnel are happily married to spouses from other countries, there are also a large number of these relationships that end in divorce.

Being stationed overseas often is accompanied by loneliness that stems from being physically separated from one's family and friends. Loneliness can often accelerate relationships, particularly in an overseas environment where the number of available people from one's own country and culture is often very limited.

Foreign partners are challenged to adapt to being married to an American whose language and culture may be quite different from their own. Being married to someone in the military poses its own unique challenges, such as multiple permanent change of stations, long periods of separation and living far from one's own family, friends and culture.

If one spouse is a foreign national, did you know each other long enough to be sure that your decision to marry was wise and properly motivated? Do you accept and embrace each other's culture? Do your respective families support your marriage? Are you in agreement about where you will live at the completion of military service?

8. One (or both) of us was married before.

While some people remarry following the death of a former spouse (particularly if they are younger), most people remarry after a divorce. Despite the loneliness that widowed and divorced people may feel, they should be careful not to rush too quickly into another marriage. Unfortunately, some people fail to recognize what contributed to their divorce and introduce problems from the previous marriage into their new relationship.

In so far as divorce rates are higher for second marriages, and even higher for third marriages, people who were married before need to be very careful about whom, when and why they remarry. Most people wait at least three years before remarrying. Remarriages that involve partners who have children need to discuss how the children will relate to their parent's new spouse and vice versa. Conflicts involving children from previous relationships are a major reason behind high remarriage divorce statistics.

If your partner or you are divorced, what was the real reason for the breakup of your marriage? Has the divorced partner structured his or her relationship with the former spouse in a way that will not interfere with the new relationship? Does a divorced partner "transfer" problems or shortcomings of a previous spouse to one's new mate? If there are children from a previous relationship living with you, is the partner who is not the mother or father of these children able to cope with the challenges involved in raising another person's child or children? A stepparent needs to realize that it may be years (and perhaps never) before a stepchild accepts him or her as a rightful member of the family.

9. We are both ethnically, racially, and linguistically the same.

Military personnel and their families who are required to travel overseas and throughout the United States come into contact with a broad variety of people representing different cultures, races, ethnic backgrounds, languages and religious beliefs. As a result of these contacts, racial and ethnically diverse marriages are generally more accepted than they are in some civilian communities.

Some families and friends, as well as people from certain areas, are more accepting than others of individuals who are different in various respects. Given the importance that loved ones play in providing a support system for married couples, it is helpful when family members and friends are not put off by such differences, but are willing to accept their loved one's partner into their lives. People who initially believe that a relationship is doomed owing to certain differences may reverse their position once they see that the couple is happily married. The arrival of children can also move non-accepting family members and friends to reconsider their stance and render support to the couple.

How do your families and friends feel about your relationship? While people should not be discriminated against based upon one's race, religion or ethnic background, do you anticipate any difficulty in being accepted? Do you anticipate that any children you might have could experience problems as a result of the particular differences in your particular relationship? Have you made efforts to "build bridges" in your relationship by learning to speak the other partner's language or prepare his or her ethnic dishes?

10. We are thoroughly briefed on the problems that can arise following a deployment.

Deployments can change people for better or for worse. One of the most challenging parts of being deployed involves being reunited after months and months of separation. By knowing how to handle the reunion phase, problems can be avoided that otherwise might harm a relationship.

Military personnel that were involved in combat operations can return home with any number of problems. Many counselors, chaplains and medical personnel are trained in post combat recovery and reintegration to help them assist returning combat veterans and spouses in dealing with a variety of psychological and physical difficulties.

In light of the fact that some combat veterans suffer from Post Traumatic Stress Disorder (PTSD) that requires professional treatment, it's helpful to be able to identify the following three types of symptoms: 1) "Intrusive" that includes flashbacks, nightmares, intrusive emotions and memories; 2) "Avoidant" that can involve avoiding relationships, emotions, responsibility for others and situations that are reminiscent of traumatic events; and 3) "Hyperarousal" often exhibited in explosive outbursts, irritability, extreme vigilance, panic symptoms and sleep disturbance.

Complications stemming from PTSD can include alcohol and drug abuse or dependence; depression and increased risk for suicide; divorce and separation; guilt; low self-esteem; chronic anxiety; phobias; and unemployment. In so far as some veterans suffer from PTSD and other problems as a result of their combat experiences, it's important to be alert for some of the above symptoms and complications that, in some cases, may not surface until six months following their return.

Catastrophically disabled veterans can receive care from the Department of Veterans Affairs (VA) whose primary mission is to provide them with medical and rehabilitative care. Organizations like the Disabled American Veterans are also available and engaged in helping wounded personnel transition into veteran status and, in many cases, from one health care system to the other.

Military personnel returning from a deployment need to recognize that changes will have occurred during their absence. A spouse may have become more independent by taking on new roles and learning new skills. Children may not only have new clothes, but new haircuts and hairstyles as well. New furniture may have been purchased and household repairs may have been completed in a manner that the service member would not have undertaken. The returning spouse must be prepared for change and should not over react against it. Frequent communication during the deployment cycle can better prepare the partners for a smooth reunion.

Adjustments will also have to be made in the marriage relationship. In so far as a spouse may have become used to doing things on his or her own, the returning service member may feel relegated to a new and less important role. Patience is needed in being reintegrated into the rhythm of family life. A lack of patience or an attempt to take charge immediately can result in resentment on the part of both the service member's spouse and children. It is important that the service member express approval, particularly in front of any children, of how his or her spouse handled matters in the course of the deployment.

Are you familiar with return and reunion classes and videos that are designed to help couples and families adjust following deployments? Are you familiar with the services provided by your chaplains, family support counselors and Military One Source?

The Survival Guide for Marriage in the Military

Biographical Profile - Man

Name:____
First MI Last
Date of Birth: _______________ Age: _____
MM / DD / YYYY

Address:____

____
City State Zip

Phones–Home:_________________Work:__________________
Cell:__________________

Email Address: _____________________________________

Occupation:____

Mother (Check one): [ ] Deceased [ ] Married to my father
[ ] Divorced [ ] Remarried
Father: (Check one): [ ] Deceased [ ] Married to my mother
[ ] Divorced [ ] Remarried

Siblings: List first names from the oldest to the youngest with their approximate ages. Follow name with designators B for brother; S for sister; HB for half-brother; HS for half-sister; SB for stepbrother; SS for stepsister. For example: John (B) 29; Mary (S) 27; Paul (HB) 22.

____
____
____
____
____

Previous Marriage(s): (Year Married/Year Divorced):
(/   ); (/   ); (/   )

Names and ages of children you fathered: ____________________

____

____

Highest Educational Level Completed (check one):

[ ] High School [ ] 2 years of College [ ] 4 years of College
[ ] Graduate School [ ] Postgraduate School

If you are employed, your personal annual income (do not include your partner's income):
[ ] 0 to $10,000 [ ] $10-25,000 [ ] $25-50,000
[ ] $50-75,000 [ ] $75-100,000 [ ] $100-150,000 [ ] $150,000+

How long have you been dating? ______________

Do you have any debts?__________________

Projected marriage date: ________________

Place:______________________________________

Type of ceremony (e.g., Justice of the Peace, Protestant, Catholic, Jewish): ____

Special circumstances prior to marriage (e.g., pregnancy, strong opposition from family or friends):

____

The Survival Guide for Marriage in the Military

Biographical Profile - Woman

Name:____

_

First MI Last

Date of Birth: __________________ Age: ______

MM / DD / YYYY

Address:____

____

City State Zip

Phones–Home:____________________Work:_____________________

Cell:____________________

Email Address: ____

Occupation:____

Mother (Check one):	[ ] Deceased	[ ] Married to my father
	[ ] Divorced	[ ] Remarried
Father: (Check one):	[ ] Deceased	[ ] Married to my mother
	[ ] Divorced	[ ] Remarried

Siblings: List first names from the oldest to the youngest with their approximate ages. Follow name with designators B for brother; S for sister; HB for half-brother; HS for half-sister; SB for stepbrother; SS for stepsister. For example: John (B) 29; Mary (S) 27; Paul (HB) 22.

____

____

____

____

____

Previous Marriage(s): (Year Married/Year Divorced):
(/   ); (/   ); (/   )

Names and ages of children you fathered: ______________________

____

____

Highest Educational Level Completed (check one):

[ ] High School [ ] 2 years of College [ ] 4 years of College
[ ] Graduate School [ ] Postgraduate School

If you are employed, your personal annual income (do not include your partner's income):
[ ] 0 to $10,000 [ ] $10-25,000 [ ] $25-50,000
[ ] $50-75,000 [ ] $75-100,000 [ ] $100-150,000 [ ] $150,000+

How long have you been dating? ______________

Do you have any debts?__________________

Projected marriage date: ________________

Place:____

Type of ceremony (e.g., Justice of the Peace, Protestant, Catholic, Jewish): ____

Special circumstances prior to marriage (e.g., pregnancy, strong opposition from family or friends):

____

STATEMENTS - MAN

(Y) = yes; (N) = no; (U) = uncertain

Review instructions for completing the inventory found on pages 19-20.

COMMUNICATION

( ) 1. *We have discussed how we will keep in touch when military requirements (e.g., deployments) force us to be separated.*

( ) 2. *Our communication skills could not be better (e.g., we never nag or employ the "silent treatment").*

( ) 3. **My partner could be more sensitive in offering me encouragement and support when I am discouraged or depressed.**

( ) 4. *My partner apologizes without hesitation after doing something wrong or hurting me.*

( ) 5. *My partner usually talks with me when there is something on his/her mind.*

( ) 6. **My partner seems uncomfortable at times in sharing his/her deep feelings with me.**

( ) 7. **I am sometimes uncomfortable in asking my partner for what I would like or want.**

( ) 8. **I am unhappy at times with the way decisions are made in our relationship.**

( ) 9. *We enjoy stimulating conversations on a broad variety of matters.*

( ) 10. **We were living together before we became engaged.**

CONFLICT RESOLUTION

( ) 1. *I generally feel satisfied with the outcome of our arguments.*

( ) 2. *We are usually able to resolve our problems without revisiting the same issues over and over again.*

( ) 3. **My partner sometimes fails to control his/her anger.**

( ) 4. *I usually can sense when and know why my partner may be upset with me.*

( ) 5. *We are able to avoid arguments over petty matters.*

( ) 6. **We sometimes bring up mistakes that were made in the past.**

( ) 7. **I am a little concerned about how a past abusive or unfaithful experience might adversely affect our relationship.**

( ) 8. **We sometimes fail to handle conflicts in constructive ways (e.g., by yelling or screaming).**

( ) 9. *My partner has never criticized me in public.*

( ) 10. *My partner and I would not hesitate to seek counseling if problems developed and persisted that threatened our relationship.*

DOLLARS AND SENSE

( ) 1. *We are familiar with our income and expenses and are committed to maintaining and following a budget.*

( ) 2. *We pay our bills on time and we agree upon who will be/is responsible for paying them.*

( ) 3. **I don't know exactly how much my partner makes and spends.**

( ) 4. *I trust my partner completely with* all of our money (e.g., checkbook, credit cards).

( ) 5. **I am uncomfortable that partner earns more than me.**

( ) 6. **We have yet to decide how much we can each spend without consulting one another.**

( ) 7. *After having discussed savings, investments, debts, assets, powers of attorneys and wills, we believe we have a sound plan for our future financial security.*

( ) 8. **We have yet to decide about the types and amount of insurance to carry (e.g., life, health, car, home).**

INTIMATE RELATIONS

( ) 1. *My partner exceeds all of my expectations for love and affection.*
( ) 2. *My partner and I are comfortable in talking about sex.*
( ) 3. *I am not worried that my partner has been or will be unfaithful.*
( ) 4. **I am sometimes uncomfortable with the way my partner relates to members of the opposite sex.**
( ) 5. **I sometimes wonder if my partner's interest in me is primarily sexual.**
( ) 6. **I sometimes worry about how my partner's past sexual relationships might have physical or other consequences in our lives.**
( ) 7. *Our relationship could end if one partner were to be unfaithful.*
( ) 8. *There are no homosexual feelings on my part or on the part of my partner.*
( ) 9. *I can easily identify at least ten different ways of maintaining intimacy and not losing romance in our relationship.*
( ) 10. *I am very well informed of various physical and psychological problems that can affect a decrease in a person's sex drive.*

TODDLER STRATEGIES

( ) 1. *We are in complete agreement about our desire to have (more) children.*
( ) 2. *We are not in total agreement about the size of family we would like to have.*
( ) 3. *We disagree about when we would like to have (more) children.*
( ) 4. **We are in agreement about methods of family planning.**
( ) 5. **We agree about how we will raise and discipline our children.**
( ) 6. *We have different views on adopting children.*
( ) 7. *We differ in our views on abortion.*

( ) 8. *We know how to help children cope with the separation of a parent (e.g., during deployments).*

( ) 9. *I am familiar with the positive and negative effects children can have upon a couple's relationship.*

IN-LAWS, OUTLAWS AND OTHERS

( ) 1. *Both of our families are supportive of our relationship.*

( ) 2. **My partner's family at times becomes too involved in our relationship.**

( ) 3. **I am uncomfortable with some of my partner's friends.**

( ) 4. **I am concerned about the degree of my partner's involvement with some of his/her friends.**

( ) 5. **I am hesitant to share with my partner some emotional hurts I experienced in my life (e.g., abuse, broken relationships).**

( ) 6. *My partner is very sensitive to any relational or emotional problems I may have experienced in the past.*

( ) 7. *We both have made a number of good friends and have similar and complementary interests.*

( ) 8. *We have a healthy balance between the time we spend together, the time we spend alone, and the time we spend with family and friends.*

( ) 9. **Some people questioned that we - may be marrying / married – too soon.**

( ) 10. *We have discussed the possibility of a parent living with us if the need were to arise.*

GREAT EXPECTATIONS

( ) 1. **I wish I knew more about my partner's past so I don't have to worry about how my partner might act in the future.**

( ) 2. *My partner and I are in agreement about leaving or staying on active duty, and we have discussed what we might do after we leave military service.*

( ) 3. *I am satisfied with how we have decided to divide our various household tasks (e.g., cooking, cleaning, paying the bills).*

( ) 4. *We have discussed and are in agreement about the issue of both partners working.*

( ) 5. *We have never had any arguments about - wedding plans / getting a divorce.*

( ) 6. *We are in agreement about what kind of home we would like to have and can afford to buy.*

( ) 7. **We cannot seem to agree about our future career plans.**

( ) 8. **Our ages are a concern to some family members and friends.**

( ) 9. **I have some doubts about - marrying / staying married to - my partner.**

( )10. *We are well prepared to deal with any number of tragedies in the future.*

DIVINE INTERVENTION

( ) 1. *We are in agreement about where – we will marry / we were married (i.e., in a civil ceremony or in a particular religious service).*

( ) 2. *I understand how a couple's moral and religious values can affect their marital success and happiness.*

( ) 3. **We have yet to agree upon the role of religion in our relationship (e.g., attending worship).**

( ) 4. **We have unresolved questions about the religious upbringing of our children.**

( ) 5. *I am satisfied with my partner's attitude toward my religious beliefs and practices.*

MISCELLANEOUS

( ) 1. **I wish my partner spent less time on the computer, watching DVDs or television.**

( ) 2. *I have never been embarrassed to be seen with my partner in public.*

( ) 3. *We agree about how neat and clean our home should be kept.*

( ) 4. **I am concerned about some of my partner's habits.**

( ) 5. *We are in agreement about the presence of pets around the house.*

( ) 6. **I wish my partner were more attentive in remembering special occasions and acknowledging them in special ways (e.g., cards, flowers, gifts).**

( ) 7. *We were both born in the United States.*

( ) 8. **One (or both) of us was married before.**

( ) 9. *We are both ethnically, racially, and linguistically the same.*

( )10. *We are thoroughly briefed on the problems that can arise following a deployment.*

Grading: Place a check mark (√) before any statement to which you answered "U" for uncertain. Then place a check mark (√) before any **bolded statement** to which you answered "Y" for yes. Finally, place a check mark (√) before any *italicized statement* to which you answered "N" for no. Those statements that you circled represent potentially problematic issues, most of which can be resolved with the help of the counseling insights provided. When you and your partner have each completed and graded your respective inventories, proceed in keeping with the Instructions on pages 19-20.

STATEMENTS - WOMAN

(Y) = yes; (N) = no; (U) = uncertain

Review instructions for completing the inventory found on pages 19-20.

COMMUNICATION

( ) 1. *We have discussed how we will keep in touch when military requirements (e.g., deployments) force us to be separated.*

( ) 2. *Our communication skills could not be better (e.g., we never nag or employ the "silent treatment").*

( ) 3. **My partner could be more sensitive in offering me encouragement and support when I am discouraged or depressed.**

( ) 4. *My partner apologizes without hesitation after doing something wrong or hurting me.*

( ) 5. *My partner usually talks with me when there is something on his/her mind.*

( ) 6. **My partner seems uncomfortable at times in sharing his/her deep feelings with me.**

( ) 7. **I am sometimes uncomfortable in asking my partner for what I would like or want.**

( ) 8. **I am unhappy at times with the way decisions are made in our relationship.**

( ) 9. *We enjoy stimulating conversations on a broad variety of matters.*

( ) 10. **We were living together before we became engaged.**

CONFLICT RESOLUTION

( ) 1. *I generally feel satisfied with the outcome of our arguments.*

( ) 2. *We are usually able to resolve our problems without revisiting the same issues over and over again.*

( ) 3. **My partner sometimes fails to control his/her anger.**

( ) 4. *I usually can sense when and know why my partner may be upset with me.*

( ) 5. *We are able to avoid arguments over petty matters.*

( ) 6. **We sometimes bring up mistakes that were made in the past.**

( ) 7. **I am a little concerned about how a past abusive or unfaithful experience might adversely affect our relationship.**

( ) 8. **We sometimes fail to handle conflicts in constructive ways (e.g., by yelling or screaming).**

( ) 9. *My partner has never criticized me in public.*

( ) 10. *My partner and I would not hesitate to seek counseling if problems developed and persisted that threatened our relationship.*

DOLLARS AND SENSE

( ) 1. *We are familiar with our income and expenses and are committed to maintaining and following a budget.*

( ) 2. *We pay our bills on time and we agree upon who will be/is responsible for paying them.*

( ) 3. **I don't know exactly how much my partner makes and spends.**

( ) 4. *I trust my partner completely with* all of our money (e.g., checkbook, credit cards).

( ) 5. **I am uncomfortable that partner earns more than me.**

( ) 6. **We have yet to decide how much we can each spend without consulting one another.**

( ) 7. *After having discussed savings, investments, debts, assets, powers of attorneys and wills, we believe we have a sound plan for our future financial security.*

( ) 8. **We have yet to decide about the types and amount of insurance to carry (e.g., life, health, car, home).**

INTIMATE RELATIONS

( ) 1. *My partner exceeds all of my expectations for love and affection.*

( ) 2. *My partner and I are comfortable in talking about sex.*

( ) 3. *I am not worried that my partner has been or will be unfaithful.*

( ) 4. **I am sometimes uncomfortable with the way my partner relates to members of the opposite sex.**

( ) 5. **I sometimes wonder if my partner's interest in me is primarily sexual.**

( ) 6. **I sometimes worry about how my partner's past sexual relationships might have physical or other consequences in our lives.**

( ) 7. *Our relationship could end if one partner were to be unfaithful.*

( ) 8. *There are no homosexual feelings on my part or on the part of my partner.*

( ) 9. *I can easily identify at least ten different ways of maintaining intimacy and not losing romance in our relationship.*

( ) 10. *I am very well informed of various physical and psychological problems that can affect a decrease in a person's sex drive.*

TODDLER STRATEGIES

( ) 1. *We are in complete agreement about our desire to have (more) children.*

( ) 2. *We are not in total agreement about the size of family we would like to have.*

( ) 3. *We disagree about when we would like to have (more) children.*

( ) 4. **We are in agreement about methods of family planning.**

( ) 5. **We agree about how we will raise and discipline our children.**

( ) 6. *We have different views on adopting children.*

( ) 7. *We differ in our views on abortion.*

( ) 8. *We know how to help children cope with the separation of a parent (e.g., during deployments).*

( ) 9. *I am familiar with the positive and negative effects children can have upon a couple's relationship.*

IN-LAWS, OUTLAWS AND OTHERS

( ) 1. *Both of our families are supportive of our relationship.*

( ) 2. **My partner's family at times becomes too involved in our relationship.**

( ) 3. **I am uncomfortable with some of my partner's friends.**

( ) 4. **I am concerned about the degree of my partner's involvement with some of his/her friends.**

( ) 5. **I am hesitant to share with my partner some emotional hurts I experienced in my life (e.g., abuse, broken relationships).**

( ) 6. *My partner is very sensitive to any relational or emotional problems I may have experienced in the past.*

( ) 7. *We both have made a number of good friends and have similar and complementary interests.*

( ) 8. *We have a healthy balance between the time we spend together, the time we spend alone, and the time we spend with family and friends.*

( ) 9. **Some people questioned that we - may be marrying / married – too soon.**

( ) 10. *We have discussed the possibility of a parent living with us if the need were to arise.*

GREAT EXPECTATIONS

( ) 1. **I wish I knew more about my partner's past so I don't have to worry about how my partner might act in the future.**

( ) 2. *My partner and I are in agreement about leaving or staying on active duty, and we have discussed what we might do after we leave military service.*

( ) 3. *I am satisfied with how we have decided to divide our various household tasks (e.g., cooking, cleaning, paying the bills).*

( ) 4. *We have discussed and are in agreement about the issue of both partners working.*

( ) 5. *We have never had any arguments about - wedding plans / getting a divorce.*

( ) 6. *We are in agreement about what kind of home we would like to have and can afford to buy.*

( ) 7. **We cannot seem to agree about our future career plans.**

( ) 8. **Our ages are a concern to some family members and friends.**

( ) 9. **I have some doubts about - marrying / staying married to - my partner.**

( )10. *We are well prepared to deal with any number of tragedies in the future.*

DIVINE INTERVENTION

( ) 1. *We are in agreement about where – we will marry / we were married (i.e., in a civil ceremony or in a particular religious service).*

( ) 2. *I understand how a couple's moral and religious values can affect their marital success and happiness.*

( ) 3. **We have yet to agree upon the role of religion in our relationship (e.g., attending worship).**

( ) 4. **We have unresolved questions about the religious upbringing of our children.**

( ) 5. *I am satisfied with my partner's attitude toward my religious beliefs and practices.*

MISCELLANEOUS

( ) 1. **I wish my partner spent less time on the computer, watching DVDs or television.**

( ) 2. *I have never been embarrassed to be seen with my partner in public.*

( ) 3. *We agree about how neat and clean our home should be kept.*

( ) 4. **I am concerned about some of my partner's habits.**

( ) 5. *We are in agreement about the presence of pets around the house.*

( ) 6. **I wish my partner were more attentive in remembering special occasions and acknowledging them in special ways (e.g., cards, flowers, gifts).**

( ) 7. *We were both born in the United States.*

( ) 8. **One (or both) of us was married before.**

( ) 9. *We are both ethnically, racially, and linguistically the same.*

( )10. *We are thoroughly briefed on the problems that can arise following a deployment.*

Grading: Place a check mark (√) before any statement to which you answered "U" for uncertain. Then place a check mark (√) before any **bolded statement** to which you answered "Y" for yes. Finally, place a check mark (√) before any *italicized statement* to which you answered "N" for no. Those statements that you circled represent potentially problematic issues, most of which can be resolved with the help of the counseling insights provided. When you and your partner have each completed and graded your respective inventories, proceed in keeping with the Instructions on pages 19-20.